The Intruders

The Invasion of Privacy
by Government and Industry

The Intruders

The Invasion of Privacy
by Government and Industry

by Senator Edward V. Long

With a Foreword by
Vice-President Hubert H. Humphrey

FREDERICK A. PRAEGER, *Publishers*
New York • Washington • London

FREDERICK A. PRAEGER, *Publishers*
111 Fourth Avenue, New York, N.Y. 10003, U.S.A.
77–79 Charlotte Street, London W.1, England

Published in the United States of America in 1967
by Frederick A. Praeger, Inc., Publishers

Library of Congress Catalog Card Number: 66-18907

PICTURE CREDITS
Photographs 3, 4, 6, 7, 10, 14 (Arthur Schatz); 5, 13 (Chuck Rapoport);
11 (Dick Meek); 12, 15 (Henry Groskinsky): *Life Magazine*

Printed in the United States of America

With grateful acknowledgment to Robert Bevan, my Legislative Assistant, and Bernard Fensterwald, Jr., Chief Counsel of the Senate Subcommittee on Administrative Practice and Procedure, for their invaluable assistance.

Foreword

Justice Brandeis, speaking about the foundations of freedom, spoke of privacy as "the right to be alone—the most comprehensive of rights, and the right most valued by civilized men."

The right to privacy includes more than simply the right to be alone. Its most important characteristic is in exercising control over the number of participants in our communications—determining whether we wish our words locked away in a diary for no eyes but our own; restricted to conversation at dinner; or blazoned in the public media.

The crucial concept, the defining right, is that individuals and groups be able to protect themselves from unwarranted invasions of their privacy.

Like most principles, it is easy to state.

The problem of making the choice of privacy as widespread and inviolable as possible is much more difficult.

Privacy's environment is continuously being changed by technological advances. Recent technological breakthroughs have made intrusion and surveillance shockingly easy to achieve and difficult to detect. Safeguards are needed if we are to protect our cherished freedoms.

The President in the summer of 1965 directed all government agencies and departments to see that wiretapping or "bugging" were not used except in cases affecting the national security. The Supreme Court in the spring of 1966 has shown a heightened interest in defining the legal limits of privacy, and Senator Long's subcommittee and other Congressional subcommittees have indicated Congressional concern.

We act differently if we believe we are being observed. If we can never be sure whether or not we are being watched and listened to, all our actions will be altered and our very character will change.

The questions raised in this book have deep significance for all of us. The answers we find will determine whether Americans in the last part of the twentieth century will be free or craven, independent or guarded.

HUBERT H. HUMPHREY

The Vice-President of the United States
Washington, D.C.

Contents

Contents

The Intruders

The Invasion of Privacy by Government and Industry

1

The Undeclared War on Privacy

ONE SUMMER DAY IN 1963, a federal agent entered a supermarket in a suburb of Kansas City, keeping close watch on a young couple who appeared to be doing their weekly grocery shopping. The couple stopped at a table where special dairy products were being shown. The young man told the two women demonstrators that he had seen one of their products, a milk substitute, advertised in the papers. He and his wife, he said, had a child who was allergic to milk. One of the demonstrators then handed him an explanatory brochure and suggested that he might wish to show it to the child's doctor.

The two demonstrators—both were moonlighting schoolteachers—could not know that their every move was being observed by a federal agent. Nor could they guess that outside the market, five more such agents were gathered around a car radio, listening to the conversation. Nor, again, that a recorder was preserving their words for possible future use. Finally, they could not know that the pleasant young parents worried about their allergic child were actually two more agents of the federal government.

This small army of government employees, equipped with electronic snooping gear, had been dispatched by the Kansas City office of the Food and Drug Administration. Its purpose was to obtain a single copy of the brochure, and to record the conversation of the demonstrators. All this, of course, at the taxpayers' expense.

The most serious crime of which the two teachers could have been accused was poor judgment in their selection of a part-time employer, a company suspected of selling a milk substitute deficient in protein. Yet so ingrained is governmental mistrust of a citizen's ability to give a straight answer to a straight question that the FDA felt compelled to send a veritable expeditionary force of snoopers. Anyone who remembers the antics of the Keystone Cops will not be surprised at the result of this expenditure of time, effort, and federal money. When the FDA later brought the company to trial—a trial based in part on the point-of-sale brochure—the jury's verdict was Not Guilty.

The experience of the two supermarket demonstrators is far from unique in America today. People in every walk of life, innocent and guilty alike, are finding themselves the targets of the eavesdropper and the busybody. Most of the prying is done by professionals who are able to make use of equipment that might even surprise someone with Ian Fleming's imagination. In this field, as in many others, modern science and technology seem to have run far ahead of man's ability to handle his new knowledge wisely.

Our space and missile programs have produced electronic advances that have revolutionized the techniques of the rubberneck. Although the greatest strides have been made with transmitters, none of the eavesdroppers' other equipment has been slighted.

On February 18, 1965, the United States Senate Subcommittee on Administrative Practice and Procedure began hearings on the activities of government agencies that invade privacy. At the first of these hearings, one of the devices viewed with special interest was an olive with a toothpick stuck in it. This ordinarily innocent object contained a tiny transmitter; the toothpick served as its antenna. Immersed in a martini, it could broadcast the length of a city block. Thus, a receiver, located anywhere within a hundred yards or so of a cocktail party, could monitor the conversation.

In addition to the olive, many other devices were on display at the Senate hearings. There were a cigarette box and a table lighter, each with a built-in transmitter. A lady's purse had a microphone built into its clasp that not only was suitable for transmitting street-corner conversation but, left conveniently behind on a desk or table, could transmit conversations taking place after its owner had gone out of the room.

The Subcommittee was also told of a device that is widely favored by those whose curiosity leads them to bug hotel and motel rooms: a picture frame that conceals a transmitter. This device is produced by one of the largest manufacturers of electronic snooping gear. It sells for a little over $200 on the open market, and is a bargain for anyone whose concept of human rights does not include privacy.

The testimony made it clear that the growing market in

transmitter devices has provided the eavesdropper with a wide-open field of operations.

For example, in an office, a transmitter can be hidden in a stapler, a lamp, a desk, or almost any other piece of equipment or furniture.

There are virtually limitless opportunities for the wide-awake snooper in household electrical appliances, as well as in furniture. The radio, the television set, and even the ordinary wall socket are especially convenient for hiding a transmitter. Power for the transmitter can be obtained from the home's electrical system, thus freeing the snooper from worry about hiding or replacing batteries.

For outdoor work, in addition to the purse transmitter, several methods have been developed for hiding these devices on the person. Men working in warm climates are able to make use of a transmitter that is suitable for wear with a sport shirt.

An ingenious appliance makes it possible for the snooper to tune in on a meeting he cannot attend. If he can lay his hands on the coat of someone who is to attend the meeting, a miniature transmitter constructed on a piece of cloth can be sewn into the lining. There is little chance that the wearer will ever discover it has been especially tailored to someone else's design.

Electronic snooping flourishes in an open marketplace. Custom-made installations can now be devised to meet the needs of any situation, and the versatility of the miniature transmitter, as well as its potential for snooping, is noteworthy. Senator Wayne Morse, of Oregon, on June 11, 1954, described to the Senate his experience as the victim of such attentions:

"Last year a secret service agent conveyed to me his belief that a microphone was hidden in my office . . . or my home. . . . The agent was able to repeat conversations which took place across my desk in the Senate building and at home."

The Senator went on to describe a scene in which he, with the help of his administrative assistant and a newspaperman, explored the office "on our hands and knees" in search of the microphone. It could not be found there, even when the FBI sent in an expert to help. The Senator continued:

"The interesting thing is that the question was asked me, 'Have you sent a lamp from your home in recent days for repair, or have you sent a chair out to be repaired?' I said, 'I do not know. Let us call Mrs. Morse.' "

Mrs. Morse, it seemed, had sent out a lamp for repair only a few days before. The microphone was never discovered, but the FBI expert pointed out that it might well have been removed after it had served its purpose.

"I cite my experience," Senator Morse said, "as an example of the kind of suspicion and fear which is developing in America these days. It shows that even a public official may be advised, 'You had better be on guard, because . . . there is, or has been, a hidden microphone in your office or home.' "

In addition to the transmitter, the eavesdropper also has available the time-tested wiretap and the conventional wired microphone, as well as the newer miniature recorder that can be concealed in a brief case or in a shoulder holster worn under a suit coat. But even these devices are now considered relatively primitive by the wizards of modern snooping science.

A one-man manufacturer of electronic equipment, one of several such operations in the country today, told the Subcommittee of a unique device which he produces that converts an ordinary telephone into a potential bug able to pick up all conversation in a room. When it is installed, the room can be monitored from any place in the United States where long-distance direct dialing is possible. The eavesdropper can overhear everything said in the bugged room until an incoming call is received or an outgoing call is placed on the telephone. Either of these actions will automatically deactivate the bug. But the snooper can, by following the original procedure, resume his monitoring immediately after such breaks in the line. With direct dialing now in general use, an eavesdropper can do his snooping thousands of miles from his victim—and at no cost, since the automatic toll-charge equipment does not record such use of the line. There is, of course, no toll record to incriminate him.

A similar, though somewhat more involved technique, was brought to the attention of Congress several years ago. It requires not only the "fixing" of the target telephone but its cross-connection to another telephone line. The snooper can then monitor the bugged room by picking up any telephone and dialing the number to which the bugged telephone has been cross-connected. This set-up allows him to hear not only conversations in the room but any conversation taking place on the cross-connected instrument.

Another device, designed to be placed inside the base of

a telephone, transmits all telephone conversations to an eavesdropper. And, when a small third wire is introduced, the instrument becomes a permanent microphone. The device is then able to transmit room conversations as well. At a Miami hearing, the Subcommittee was given evidence of an improvement on these techniques. A Florida company manufactures a small, clear-plastic piece, similar to the one found inside each telephone mouthpiece, that contains a tiny transmitter. It takes only a few seconds to exchange the two pieces, and then even an amateur can tap a telephone.

With a fine show of democracy, these modern devices are used to pry out corporate as well as personal secrets. An experience of Schenley Industries, Inc., confirms this. Officers of the company had been working for some time on confidential plans for future operations. However, bits and pieces of these closely guarded plans began to come back to the president of the corporation from outside sources. Suspecting the use of wiretaps or bugs, he decided to call in experts with the latest in detection equipment.

The technicians began their search in the Florida home of the company's president. In the study, where many confidential business conferences had been held, they discovered a small transmitter concealed in the bar. The device was still broadcasting when found. The search also revealed a tap on the lines leading to the president's private office telephone, which had been converted into a microphone that picked up everything said in his office. The eavesdropper had total coverage of all conversations in the president's office, including his personal as well as business telephone calls.

It might be concluded that, to insure a private, unrecorded conversation, persons must talk in a rowboat in the middle of a lake, dressed in swimsuits. But even these precautions will not stop the eavesdropper who knows his business. He can always use the parabolic microphone or the telescope microphone, capable of picking up distant conversation.

The Subcommittee investigation has established that purchases of such equipment have been made by official agencies at all levels of government, by private detectives, and by anyone else willing to pay for it. Mass marketing has brought many expensive items down to prices low enough for them to be enjoyed by the average citizen. Unfortunately, this merchandising advance has also benefited snoopers. The cost of many of these devices was originally high, but mass-marketing techniques, also used by the distributors of imported devices, have made prices of some items quite reasonable.

Richard Gerstein, District Attorney of Dade County, Florida, displayed before the Subcommittee a wide selection of such equipment purchased without difficulty. Included were telephone transmitting devices, bug transmitters, wireless microphones, and a series of different types of room bugs. All devices had been purchased either by telephone or across the counter. "With the exception of one shop owner," Gerstein said, "who stated that the equipment would only be sold to persons having identification as private investigators, there were no questions asked."

Ralph Ward, Vice President of Mosler Research Products, a manufacturer of electronic snooping devices, testified that his company's distribution was somewhat more restricted: "For ten years, our distribution was limited to law-enforcement agencies." But then, he said, "About two years ago, we opened this up to sell to law-enforcement agencies *and licensed detectives, mainly because the field is spreading into industry now* [italics added]."

Even with this vast array of new equipment to choose from, many eavesdroppers find the older methods useful. A special agent of the Internal Revenue Service, recognized as its technical specialist in the Boston area, testified in 1965 that some of his activities were a practical blend of the old and the new. He had received training in the use of "technical investigative aids," at a school run by the Treasury Department. The very existence of this school introduces a curiously paradoxical note: Since 1938, the IRS has prohibited wiretapping, by specific regulation. Despite this, it has trained at least 125 of its agents in the installation and use of wiretaps.

The Boston electronics man went to work for the IRS in 1961. In the next four years, he installed numerous wiretaps and bugs, not only for his own agency but for others as well. For instance, in 1962, U.S. Treasury agents called on him to help with a betting-tax investigation in the Boston suburbs. Employing the ingenuities so carefully taught him at the Department school, he picked the lock of an office that was under suspicion, entered, and installed a tap.

It should be of some concern to the citizens of a country that produced the Declaration of Independence, among other documents attesting to man's struggle for individual freedom, that in this case alone their government's agents violated the United States Constitution, Massachusetts criminal law, and the IRS's own regulations.

And what was accomplished by these violations? In the agent's own words, "Nothing came of this. It was unsuccessful."

In another betting-tax case, this same specialist went to work with a pen register. This is a small device developed to record the numbers dialed by a particular telephone. It is attached to the telephone line exactly like a wiretap. However, rather than recording conversations, it merely prints a tape listing the numbers called. This kind of information helps to determine what contacts have been made by those using the telephone under surveillance.

This same man was also adept at installing bugs. In June, 1962, he concealed a microphone in a conference room at the IRS offices in Boston. He explained to the Subcommittee that the microphone was not installed for the purpose of overhearing conversations between lawyers and their taxpayer clients while they were alone in the the room. To the best of his knowledge, it had never been so used. Other testimony indicated, however, that the bug came close to being used for that purpose on at least one occasion.

On July 26, 1965, the Commissioner of Internal Revenue himself submitted to the Subcommittee a list of twenty-two cities in which concealed microphones had been installed in IRS conference rooms. In May, he had ordered the removal of all permanent installations. But he did not prohibit the installation of hidden microphones in conference rooms for specific interviews. In other words, it was a case of *this will never happen again—except when I think it necessary.*

The bugs and wiretaps of this Boston specialist do not add up to a great many over a four-year period, but one must consider the number of people whose conversations were aired at each installation. Also, this list concerns only one technician out of 125 similarly skilled persons that the IRS has at its disposal. When one realizes that the IRS is only one of the many investigative agencies on the federal level alone, the individual citizen is justified in his measure of concern and moral outrage, especially if he remembers those values for which our country is supposed to stand.

One federal agency, the Federal Bureau of Investigation, has publicly admitted its use of wiretapping year after year. During the past few years, it has usually acknowledged fewer than a hundred taps in operation on the reporting date. Assurances have always been given that these are limited to national-security matters and kidnaping cases, where human life is in danger. Assurances have also been given that each tap is authorized in writing by the Attorney General.

The FBI's use of bugs, however, does not seem to have been so strictly limited. The Division Security Supervisor of the Southwestern Bell Telephone Company told the Senate Subcommittee at a hearing in Kansas City that, on two occasions in 1961, the telephone company received requests from the FBI for the installation of certain leased lines. Such lines function, in effect, as private direct lines between two locations. In response to the first request, two direct lines were set up between the local FBI office and a telephone pole at the rear of a night club. In response to the other request, a direct line was put in between the FBI office and a local shop. In the second case, a public telephone was installed just outside the shop, and an extra line was run to it for use by the FBI.

The Bell Telephone supervisor testified that he understood these arrangements were made in connection with gambling investigations. With the use of appropriate listening devices tied to the leased lines, the FBI was in a position to do its monitoring from the convenience of its own offices. It was also the supervisor's understanding that these installations had been approved by the Attorney General. The Bell Telephone employee revealed at least nine other instances in which leased lines had been set up at the request of the FBI. One of these did actually involve national security.

According to the witness, the telephone company did not have a similar arrangement with any other federal agency. But he substantiated earlier testimony that special company information valuable for wiretapping would, on occasion, be made available to the Kansas City Police Department in cases of kidnaping, blackmail, or other crimes where human life was threatened.

This revelation of FBI bugging was substantiated in July, 1966, when the United States Solicitor General filed a memorandum with the Supreme Court admitting that "for a period of years prior to 1963, and continuing into 1965" the FBI had used bugging devices in the interest of internal security or national safety, which included the investigation of organized crime.

As with the IRS Boston man, the number of eavesdropping installations revealed here does not appear large for a five-year period. But again we are dealing with only one government agency out of many, and the specific office is only one of many in that agency. Then, of course, there is no way to be sure that in any of these investigations the whole story has ever been told. By its very nature, eavesdropping flourishes underground; it turns away from the public light and is nourished in maximum secrecy. In view of this, the Subcommittee has been fortunate to unearth as many witnesses as it has.

We are entitled to ask a few questions at this point. For instance: Who have been the victims of this electronic shadowing? Whose privacy has been invaded by the seemingly inexhaustible variety of listening devices?

Here are some answers: In Kansas City, the victims were gambling suspects and two schoolteachers. In Washington, D.C., it was Senator Wayne Morse. In Miami, it was the president of a large corporation. In Boston, it was suspected tax-law violators. And this is only a sampling of the number and variety of Americans who have been spied upon by public and private agents.

The guilty and the innocent alike have shared the anonymous attentions of snoopers. The famous and the infamous, the rich and the poor, the most respected and the least—all may come within range of a secret ear. In 1961, in Baton Rouge, Louisiana, the telephones of a rabbi, a Baptist minister, and the local director of the American Friends Service Committee were tapped. These three generally respected men had committed the crime—in someone's judgment—of trying to improve racial understanding.

Innocence is not necessarily a safeguard against eavesdropping, nor is physical security. The most carefully guarded family in our country is that of the President, and yet there have been stories of wiretaps on telephones used for personal calls by members of the first family. In the mid-1930's, the New York City police found themselves tapped into a telephone line that was assigned to the wife of President Roosevelt. This time it was a mistake: The tappers were aiming at a suspected member of Murder Incorporated. However, Willis Adams, who served with Army Intelligence during World War II, told an even more startling story on an NBC television program in October, 1965. During the war, he had been for a time in charge of an intelligence team operating in Chicago, and he described the widespread tapping and bugging activities of this group. It had wired almost every hotel in Chicago, according to Adams. The most prominent victim of its eavesdropping activities, he said, was Mrs. Franklin D. Roosevelt when she visited that area.

Under orders, the Adams team had secured the entire neighborhood around the Argonne Laboratory. This included the tapping and bugging of hotel rooms occupied by lab personnel. Listening devices were placed in the working areas and in the women's and men's restrooms. Twenty-four-hour-a-day surveillance was maintained on five persons involved in the project, two of whom were Enrico Fermi and J. Robert Oppenheimer. All this was done in connection with the development of the atomic bomb. Of course, security was essential, but the Adams story raises unsettling questions as to the methods used to insure it.

A news story of 1965 (UPI, August 19) indicates, incidentally, that our country has no monopoly on eavesdropping at the highest level. It was revealed that a telephone in a home where Queen Elizabeth of England and the Queen Mother had been guests was monitored.

But Presidents, royalty, scientists, Senators, and business executives do not begin to occupy all the time and attention of the snooper. The Miami District Attorney informed the Subcommittee that "From the number of complaints presented to my office, I would estimate that one of every three contested divorce cases involves the use of tapped telephones and intercepted conversation."

One example of eavesdropping that touches a vast number of Americans was related to the Subcommittee by Joseph Beirne, President of the Communications Workers of America. He revealed that the telephone company does not limit its invasions of privacy to assisting the FBI and other government tappers. He pointed out that "as part of its training program, and as part of its continuing close supervision of its employees, the telephone industry has developed equipment for monitoring its operators, its service assistants, its commercial office employees—in short, all of its employees who deal with the customer. Such monitoring means, of course, that the customer is, in effect, monitored at the same time."

Switchboard operators can normally be monitored at several levels of supervisory control, and recordings can be made of the operator's conversation with the customer. The company also conceals microphones to monitor employees who have direct contact with customers. Beirne: "If you go to a telephone business office to pay your bill or request a service change, or for any other purpose, your conversation probably will be monitored.

"Typically, a small desk calendar will be the device which will hide a secret microphone capable of picking up every word you and the employee say to each other." He warned, "If she is pretty, gentlemen, do not ask her for a date. The supervisor who is monitoring her may object."

According to Beirne, the monitoring equipment developed by the telephone industry for use on its own employees has been sold to industrial firms. As an example, he reported that a hospital administrator had been dismissed from his job for monitoring, among other conversations, confidential talks between doctor and patient. Other users of such equipment have included airlines, department stores, and even a restaurant. In the last case, hidden microphones were installed under each table. The management solemnly maintained that this operation was necessary to check on employee courtesy toward the customers.

In the spring of 1966, the Subcommittee established that the telephone company had for years gone beyond mere monitoring of conversations between its employees and its customers. In major cities it maintained monitoring rooms where telephone conversations, picked at random, were systematically monitored. The alleged purpose was for quality control. The extent of this monitoring, which was discontinued on June 1, 1966, was so great (39 million telephone conversations in 1965) that practically every American must have been monitored at least once.

Thorough as wiretaps and bugs may be, today's invasions of privacy by no means stop with them. Law-enforcement officials continue to use traditional methods of search and seizure, and mail covers. First-class mail has been opened, and peepholes used to watch postal employees at work and in their dressing rooms. Until the summer of 1965, the federal government conducted a program of monitoring and holding incoming foreign mail suspected of being propaganda. Modern technology has brought forth another threat to privacy in the computer. Now all kinds of information, some of it quite personal and even intimate, is being fed into these machines that never forget.

Private business, as well as the government, makes use of computers. Also, like the government, business has expanded its use of lie detectors and psychological testing. Equipped with these two instruments, the "brain-watchers" are able to probe deeply into the most privately held secrets. Two-way mirrors are a common tool of industry and government. Whether a person is shopping at the counter of a store, trying on clothing in a dressing room, or talking with his lawyer in a government conference room, he may well be under surveillance through a two-way mirror.

Why is it that the devices and methods mentioned here are used in a democracy that professes to respect the dignity of the individual? One partial answer was supplied a long time ago in another country. In 1872, during a discussion of the Code of Criminal Procedure for India, the question arose as to why the police would occasionally torture a prisoner. An experienced civil officer observed, "There is a great deal of laziness in it. It is far pleasanter to sit comfortably in the shade rubbing red pepper into a poor devil's eyes than to go about in the sun hunting up evidence."

Laziness is a poor enough excuse for the delinquent acts of a private person or group. But we are dealing here with the acts of government agencies as well. In the eyes of many people throughout the world, America has represented the universal dream of the inviolability of the individual. We are entitled to ask, therefore, if we have now come to a time when this liberty is to be sacrificed merely to indulge the presumed laziness of certain government functionaries.

2

"...the right to be let alone"

WHAT IS PRIVACY, and why is it important to us?

This question answers itself once we look at a society where privacy was systematically attacked and all but eliminated. Under Hitler and the Nazis, the destruction of the individual's sense of his own privacy was one of the principal methods used to gain total state control over the German people. Wiretapping and electronic eavesdropping were high on the list of techniques used by the Gestapo. No one was safe from the listening ears of the secret police. Visitors to a German home were sometimes taken into the bathroom to exchange comments in whispers, because this was the most difficult room to tap. Diplomats and officials—and private citizens as well—met in public parks to escape eavesdroppers. Even after World War II had started, Berliners steered clear of telephones when they wanted to talk freely.

Another routine Gestapo technique was the predawn arrest. There was the unannounced bang on the door, the invasion of the home, and the dragging or driving of people in their night clothes into the streets. This kind of brutal invasion of privacy was designed to achieve the maximum in intimidation and fear. Mass raids were conducted regularly in this manner in Germany and, later, all over conquered Europe.

The situation in Germany was appraised by Dr. E. K. Bramstedt, who wrote in his book *Dictatorship and Political Police:* "The general atmosphere resulting from the operations of the secret police is pregnant with uncertainty, fear, suspicion, and readiness to pin the onus for all troubles on one's neighbors. This atmosphere can be summed up in the formula: 'No private life permitted.' As Dr. Ley once said: 'There is no such thing as privacy for the individual in National Socialist Germany. The only person who still enjoys some privacy in Germany is someone who is asleep.' "

Under a ruling of the German Supreme Court, criticism of the regime was not allowed even in private conversation between husband and wife. Gestapo Chief Heinrich Himmler stated that "Carping and criticisms are permitted only to those who are not afraid of the concentration camp." It was a brave man who criticized the state, even when talking to himself.

Nazi Germany was a society in which privacy was, for all practical purposes, nonexistent. When the individual was not actually under surveillance, he was always possessed by the fear that he might be. Along with this was the fear that the secret police might descend on him at any time. The German citizen had only one right under Hitler: to serve the regime with his entire being.

The traditional relationship between the citizen and his

government in the United States differs markedly from that of the Nazi state, both in concept and practice. In 1928, Justice Louis Brandeis said of this relationship:

> The makers of our Constitution undertook to secure conditions favorable to the pursuit of happiness. They recognized the significance of man's spiritual nature, of his feelings and of his intellect. They knew that only a part of the pain, pleasure, and satisfactions of life are to be found in material things. They sought to protect Americans in their beliefs, their thoughts, their emotions, and their sensations. They conferred, as against the Government, the right to be let alone—the most comprehensive of rights and the right most valued by civilized men. To protect that right, every unjustifiable intrusion by the Government upon the privacy of the individual, whatever the means employed, must be deemed a violation of the Fourth Amendment.

Justice Brandeis put his finger on the critical distinction between a police state and a democracy. It is the right of privacy: the right to be let alone, not only at home, but at the office, at church, and in associations with others for whatever purpose.

Many people seem to take a double view of this right. They assert the right to be let alone by their neighbors, business competitors, and other essentially private individuals. But when the law enforcer intrudes, they say, "The innocent have nothing to fear. I don't mind if government investigators listen to my telephone calls, bug my conversations, or search me and my premises. I have nothing to hide." They seem unconcerned by government use of techniques that invade privacy. But is the right of privacy so conveniently divisible? Can the citizen allot one fragment to the government while holding firmly to another, and still continue to maintain that his life is "private"?

Personal inviolability, particularly with respect to the home, is a concept that has concerned some of the finest minds in the history of Western civilization. Here is William Pitt, the Elder, speaking in 1763: "The poorest man may in his cottage bid defiance to all the force of the Crown. It may be frail; its roof may shake; the wind may blow through it; the storms may enter, the rain may enter —but the King of England cannot enter; all his forces dare not cross the threshold of the ruined tenement."

There are references to this right in Justinian's sixth-century code of Roman laws and, in pre-Christian Rome, in the writings of Cicero. In fact, it is from the Romans that the concept of the individual's right to privacy came into Western thought. The sanctuary offered by the home under Roman law appears in some ways to have been more impressive than our own: even when subject to arrest, a man could not, under the law, be dragged from his home.

Concern for privacy has played a crucial role in our history, and the struggle for this right made its formal debut in a courtroom in Boston, in 1761.

The Superior Court of Massachusetts Bay was considering an application for a writ of assistance filed by Charles Paxton, Collector of Customs in Boston. This writ would authorize Paxton and his deputies to command any and all law-enforcement officers to enter any home or office and search it from top to bottom, if they suspected it might contain goods on which import duties had not been paid. The writ contained no safeguard against its arbitrary application. Once issued, Paxton and his successors would never have to appear before the court to answer for its use. In effect, the writ of assistance would grant the Collector of Customs and his men absolute power.

The merchants of Boston took steps to challenge the request in open court, and were represented by James Otis, one of the ablest members of the Boston bar. He told the court:

> I take this opportunity to declare that whether under a fee or not (for in such a cause as this I despise a fee) I will to my dying day oppose with all the powers and facilities God has given me, all such instruments of slavery on the one hand, and villainy on the other, as this writ of assistance is. . . . The writ . . . being general, is illegal. It is a power that places the liberty of every man in the hands of every petty officer. . . . Now one of the most essential branches of English liberty is the freedom of one's house. . . . This writ . . . would totally annihilate this privilege. Custom-house officers may enter our houses, when they please; we are commanded to permit them entry. Their menial servants may enter, may break locks, bars, and everything in their way; and whether they break through malice or revenge, no man, no court, can inquire. . . . Thus reason and the Constitution are against this writ. . . .

John Adams, who was to become our second President, was in the courtroom, and many years later he wrote that "American independence was then and there born; the seeds of patriots and heroes were then and there sown. . . . Every man of a crowded audience appeared to me to go away, as I did, ready to take arms against writs of assistance."

The Otis argument in defense of privacy did not persuade the Massachusetts court, but it was of extreme importance to the American cause, and provided a solid legal base for opposing writs of assistance in other colonies. More important, it struck the first significant blow for freedom from England. Thus, the first milestone on the road to independence was the right to be let alone, the right to be free from arbitrary intrusion by the government into the home.

The experience of the American colonists with the instruments of tyranny led them to make sure that their new government would not intrude into the sanctity of the home or the privacies of life. At least seven of the thirteen original states included in their constitutions a ban on unreasonable search and seizure. Later, a number of states made it a condition of their ratification of the U.S. Constitution that a Bill of Rights be adopted. Protection against writs of assistance and general warrants (which placed no limit on the object of search and seizure) was one of the guarantees demanded.

Article IV of the Bill of Rights (the Fourth Amendment), approved in 1791, stated that, "The right of the people to be secure in their persons, houses, papers, and effects, against unreasonable searches and seizures, shall not be violated, and no warrants shall issue but upon probable cause, supported by oath or affirmation, and particularly describing the place to be searched, and the persons or things to be seized."

After nearly two hundred years, it would seem that the area of protection would be clearly defined, but legal history shows that it is not. One of the primary reasons for this is the language of the Fourth Amendment. It was not intended to provide a right to absolute privacy. Instead, it sets out specific requirements for a lawful warrant and prohibits unreasonable searches and seizures. That single word "unreasonable" has opened the way for frequent differences of opinion and even controversy.

The official interests that led the British crown to the use of writs of assistance and general warrants still exist. Taxes must be collected, and the government must be protected against overthrow by illegal means. Also, criminal law must be enforced. The welfare of society requires that each of these tasks be carried out fully and effectively. In discharging their responsibilities over the years, law-enforcement officials have often come in conflict with the right of privacy.

These conflicts have tended to divide the American people into two schools: those who lean toward law enforcement and those who lean toward individual privacy as having the greater value. The composition of the two groups at any one time depends upon the particular governmental interest involved. Support for the government interest reaches its maximum strength where national security is involved. Where the issue is criminal law enforcement that does not involve national security, fewer people stress the government's claims. The least support for the official interest, as might be expected, comes when the issue is the collection of taxes. But regardless of which attitude a person tends to favor in a specific case, he may be able to call upon the language of the Fourth Amendment to support his position.

In view of conflicts of interest and the pressures on privacy, what is the state of the law today?

Congress has proceeded with caution in authorizing searches and seizures. For more than a century, it followed a case-by-case approach, authorizing search warrants for specific purposes in a number of acts. But despite this caution, the Supreme Court in 1886, in *Boyd* vs. *United States,* held that one such authorization violated the Fourth Amendment. The offending statute did not, strictly speaking, authorize a search warrant. It authorized the courts in certain cases, on the motion of the government, to demand of the defendant that he produce specific business books and papers that would tend to prove the government's case. If a defendant refused, the statute provided that the allegations as to what the documents might prove be taken as if confessed.

The Supreme Court's decision in this case is significant. It said: "It is not the breaking of his doors, and the rummaging of his drawers, that constitutes the essence of the offense, but it is the invasion of his indefeasible right of personal security, personal liberty, and private property. . . . Breaking into a house and opening boxes and drawers are circumstances of aggravation; but any forcible and compulsory extortion of a man's own testimony or his private papers to be used as evidence to convict him of crime or to forfeit his goods, is within the condemnation of [this] judgment."

In the Boyd case, the Court found the statute required unreasonable search and seizure, because it demanded the production of private papers where the sole interest of the government was to use them as evidence. The Court did not weigh the need of society to collect taxes against the right of privacy. Instead, it determined that the men who framed the Constitution considered paper searches and seizures unreasonable. It held that the Amendment, therefore, prohibited all such government actions, regardless of the interest involved. With this decision, the Court breathed life into the Fourth Amendment.

It was not until World War I that Congress made search warrants generally available for use in criminal prosecution. And even today, the statutory authority remains quite specific. Warrants may be obtained only where there is probable cause to believe a specific thing can be found at a certain place. In line with the Boyd decision, warrants can be issued only to search for and seize certain things—fruits of crime, instruments of crime, contraband, and goods upon which duties have not been paid. In such cases the government has a legal interest in possession of the item superior to that of the individual. Warrants cannot be obtained to seize mere evidence of a crime. That is, a warrant cannot be obtained to search for a bloody shirt, or for private papers that speak of a crime that has been committed.

A look at the vicissitudes to which the right of privacy has been subject may be helpful in forming a just picture of the present situation. Before 1949, actions of state legislatures and state officers were not held subject to the Fourth Amendment. Each state was free to draw the line between its own authority and the privacy of its inhabitants. Then, in 1949, the Supreme Court, in *Wolf* vs. *Colorado,* held that the protection of the Fourth Amendment is basic to a free society. It is thus enforceable against the states through the due process clause of the Fourteenth Amendment, which reads: "No State shall make or enforce any law which shall abridge the privileges or immunities of citizens of the United States, nor shall any State deprive any person of life, liberty, or property without due process of law, nor deny to any person within its jurisdiction the equal protection of the law."

The decision in the Wolf case had only partial effect on the states, because the Supreme Court refused to go all the way in applying the Fourth Amendment. In 1914, in *Weeks* vs. *United States,* it had held that evidence obtained by unreasonable search and seizure was inadmissible in federal court. But, in Wolf, it did not make this rule applicable to state courts. It was thus left to each state to determine for itself whether it would allow the use of unlawfully seized evidence. Many states continued, therefore, to ignore the source of evidence. As a result, the right of privacy of individuals continued to differ markedly from state to state.

However, in 1961, in *Mapp* vs. *Ohio,* the Supreme Court took a major step in making the right of privacy uniform throughout the nation. Here it held that the Fourteenth Amendment required the application of the Weeks evidence rule to the states as well. Two years later, in *Kerr* vs. *California,* the Court held that "the standard of reasonableness" for judging searches and seizures is the same under the Fourth and Fourteenth Amendments. Both federal and state governments must now conform to the same standards of conduct. As a result, the right of privacy no longer suffers such obvious differences from state to state and, since evidence obtained by unreasonable searches and seizures is no longer admissible anywhere, the open temptation to law-enforcement officers to violate the Fourth Amendment has been removed.

In construing the Fourth Amendment, where has the Supreme Court drawn the line protecting privacy?

Searches of business places, garages, and vehicles, as well as homes, are covered by the Amendment. Persons occupying hotel or motel rooms, and guests in private homes are entitled to its protection. The Amendment also protects letters sent through the mails. Federal officers may not break down a door to effect a lawful arrest or seizure, unless they are refused admission after giving audible notice of their authority and purpose. Of course, this formal notice is unnecessary when the person opening the door recognizes the officers and bars their entry because he knows their purpose. The notice also may not be required where there is a need to rescue a victim in peril, and where destruction of evidence is imminent.

The primary thrust of the Fourth Amendment has been to protect privacy by placing a judicial officer between the police and the individual. But despite this, searches can be made without a warrant when they are part of a lawful arrest. This has been one of the most troublesome areas for the Supreme Court in distinguishing between privacy and the authority of the government.

It has long been recognized that an officer can search a person when he places him under arrest. This is obviously necessary to protect the officer against attack by use of a concealed weapon. In more recent years, the authority to search has been extended to the area under control of the arrested person, and it is this that has brought about the conflict.

The Court in 1931 and 1932 invalidated searches of desks and files in the room of an arrested person. Conversely, in 1947, it approved a five-hour search of a four-room apartment as incident to a lawful arrest. In this case, it approved the seizure of Selective Service registration cards found in a sealed envelope, even though they had nothing to do with the crime for which the arrest was made. In 1948, the Court lessened the effectiveness of this decision by holding that, if it were feasible to obtain a warrant, a search without a warrant was illegal, even as part of a lawful arrest. But then, in 1950, the Court approved an extended search of a one-room office which was conducted as part of an arrest. In 1957, it considered a case in which federal officers armed with an arrest warrant for one person, arrested three persons and seized papers found on them, as well as the contents of a cabin in which they were living. The Court found this seizure invalid.

In May of 1957, a recently defected Russian spy informed the FBI that he had cooperated for several years with another Russian agent, Rudolph Abel, who lived at a small New York hotel. At the time, the defector refused to be a public witness, choosing to cooperate only in secret. Without his testimony, it was felt that the government did not have sufficient evidence to justify an arrest and indictment of Abel. In June, the FBI notified the Immigration Service of Abel's identity and address, and the Service decided to arrest him with an administrative warrant as a preliminary to deportation. The FBI accompanied the

Immigration officers to the hotel where the arrest was made.

After Abel had been taken away, the FBI searched the vacated room. The men found a hollow pencil containing microfilm, and a block of wood containing a "cipher pad." Abel had thrown these into a wastebasket while packing.

At Abel's trial, the evidence picked up by the FBI was used against him, along with that seized in the course of the actual arrest. By the narrow margin of a five to four decision, the Supreme Court upheld the use of this evidence, the FBI seizures being approved on the basis that the items found in the basket were "abandoned property."

The dissenters to this decision were concerned over the use of an administrative warrant to support a search. In such a case, a judicial officer is not involved either before or after the arrest or search. Grave danger to personal liberty was foreseen in the precedent established by the approval of this search.

A search warrant permits the seizure of the specific item described in the warrant. In a search that takes place during a lawful arrest, there is no real limitation to what the officer may pick up and take along. Judge Learned Hand was once faced with a case in which, as incident to an arrest, papers had been seized though not designated by a previously obtained search warrant. To approve such a search, Judge Hand felt, would be equivalent to an admission that a person's papers would be secure only so long as he stayed away from home. It would also turn all lawful arrests into general warrants, and this is specifically condemned by the Fourth Amendment. The judge warned: "Nor should we forget that what seems fair enough against a squalid huckster of bad liquor may take on a very different face, if used by a government determined to suppress political opposition under the guise of sedition."

Another legally troublesome area is the question of "probable cause." An officer must show probable cause to a judicial officer to obtain a search warrant or an arrest warrant, and he must have probable cause to make a lawful arrest without a warrant. There has been agreement on one point: "A search is not to be made legal by what it turns up." That is, things seized cannot be used to show probable cause for the arrest or search. The legality of the action must be based on information known before the search.

Particularly in recent years, information obtained from paid informers has been used by law-enforcement officers as a basis for probable cause. The Supreme Court has upheld the use of such information to support probable cause where the officer has found the informer reliable from past experience, and where there is some independent supporting information. These qualifications have led to differing opinions and split decisions. In one case, an officer, acting on word from an informer, smelled opium coming from a room before he entered it and found the accused. The arrest was held unlawful. In another case, a federal agent, again acting on word from an informer, arrested a suspect when the only independent information he had concerned his physical appearance: he fit the informer's description. The Supreme Court upheld this arrest and search.

While arrests can be made without a warrant if probable cause exists, the Court has held that "it is settled doctrine that probable cause for belief that certain articles subject to seizure are in a dwelling cannot of itself justify a search without a warrant. The decisions of this Court have time and again underscored the essential purpose of the Fourth Amendment to shield the citizen from unwarranted intrusions into his privacy."

The foregoing provides only a sketch of the Supreme Court's judgments in connection with search and seizure. As indicated, the Court has generally tried to preserve the area of privacy which the framers of the Fourth Amendment intended to protect. On the other hand, it has recognized the practical difficulties facing law-enforcement officers. On occasion, the decisions seem to have leaned rather far in upholding their actions. But law-enforcement officers—as well as many others—tend to feel that the decisions have also, on occasion, leaned far in the other direction.

For the most part, the Court has remembered that the rights of the innocent as well as the guilty are at stake and, because of its decisions, Americans still enjoy a substantial area of privacy. The line may not always be clear, but it is there.

The Griswold case, brought before the Court in 1965, was one involving a unique type of invasion of privacy. Here, the instrument of intrusion was the Connecticut statute that banned the use of birth-control devices. In a seven to two decision, the Court held that the law violated the due process clause of the Fourteenth Amendment (see p. 30). From this decision it would appear that there is a constitutional right to privacy, separate and apart from that provided by the Fourth Amendment. This judgment greatly strengthened the right of privacy, but it is difficult to foresee its consequences.

In the days when the Constitution was written, the methods of invasion of privacy were direct and sometimes even brutal. Arrests and physical searches and seizures made up the bulk of the invasions. In these cases, the victim was fully aware of the officer's actions, and could take some steps to correct the situation. The private citizen, then, had at least a reasonable opportunity to take what shelter he could under the provisions of the Constitution.

And then came electricity! Its uses, which have simplified so much of life for so many, have opened up a whole empire of enterprise for the invader of individual privacy. Nowadays, the victim hardly stands a chance.

In 1837, Samuel F. B. Morse invented the telegraph, and no sooner did it become operational than the wiretapper was born. California found it necessary to pass a law against wiretapping in 1862, and two years later one of the pioneer tappers was arrested under the statute. He was part of a conspiracy to intercept news of stock operations and sell the information. During the Civil War, certain soldiers were trained to wiretap for the purpose of obtaining military intelligence. Some of these men, like their counterparts in later wars, found their training of help in securing employment in civilian life. They had learned a trade.

One of the major uses of wiretapping after the Civil War, and into the early 1900's, was to intercept news stories. The development of the telephone during these years merely added a new area of operation. Indignation over the interception of news led to legislation in Illinois in

1895, and in California in 1905, to prohibit telephone wiretapping. New York, in 1916, was the site of the first sensational wiretap scandal involving law-enforcement officers. The mayor had authorized the police to tap the conversations of five Catholic priests to obtain evidence in an investigation of charity frauds. In the resulting controversy, it was revealed that the local police had been wiretapping since 1895 with the cooperation of the telephone company. The *New York Times* supported the police with an editorial that included this comment: "The *Times* feels too few wires have been tapped, not too many, and that the exposé has hurt the cause of justice."

The Supreme Court and the other courts have had notable difficulty in trying to clarify the area of wiretapping, bugging, and the ever more refined electronic developments. These techniques have introducd a new concept of privacy invasion, further complicating an already difficult area. The thing seized in such cases is conversation, and the seizure may not involve physical entry, if the appropriate technique is used.

The Court has not re-examined wiretapping under the Fourth Amendment since 1928. This is because Congress enacted a law in 1934 that prohibits wiretapping and the divulgence of evidence so obtained, and the Court has decided all subsequent wiretap cases on the basis of this law or related decisions.

Today the situation is this: the Fourth Amendment, as construed by the Court, provides no protection against invasion by government agents through wiretapping or bugging—unless the agents are so careless as to be guilty of an actual physical intrusion of some sort. With this one exception, the Constitution under past Court decisions presents no bar to government electronic snooping on any of us at any time, regardless of individual innocence or guilt. There is no requirement of reasonableness, no judicial officer, nor does probable cause have to be shown. Fortunately for us, the situation is somewhat alleviated by federal and state laws. Justice Brandeis pointed out in his dissent in the Olmstead case that, "As a means of espionage, writs of assistance and general warrants are but puny instruments of tyranny and oppression when compared with wiretapping." And since 1928, when he wrote those words, we are all far more vulnerable.

Today, there are about ninety million telephones in operation in this country alone. The U.S. has approximately half the telephones there are in the world. And 97 per cent of all the world's telephones can be interconnected. For this reason, a tap, though it is placed on a single telephone, potentially affects almost all of them. Placed on a suspect's phone, the tap monitors both ends of all calls he makes or receives, without regard for which of the millions of available telephones he may be connected to. Completely innocent and irrelevant conversations are, of course, intercepted as well as any that may be incriminating.

Our courts have recognized that certain conversations have a special right to secrecy; conversations between man and wife, doctor and patient, minister and parishioner, lawyer and client, all are traditionally inviolate. But this traditional protection collapses completely before the devious attentions of the snooper. The government wiretapper has never shown any special inclination to avoid the interception of such calls. In fact, doctors and lawyers have been among his favorite victims. In 1961, a law-enforcement official told a Senate subcommittee that the police should be given authority to tap in criminal abortion cases. But if a suspected doctor's telephone was to be tapped, his conversations with *all* patients are bound to be overheard. All these doctor-patient communications would be intercepted and carefully recorded, *and the doctor could well be completely innocent of the suspected illegal practice.*

In 1949, the FBI maintained a wiretap on the telephone of an accused woman, both before and during her trial. The agents were thus able to overhear the discussion of trial strategy with her attorney. In these circumstances, the government has the benefit of advance and inside information with respect to the defense.

Even where caution is exercised, a tap cannot distinguish between a privileged and a nonprivileged conversation. Few people would be reassured by the news that the listening officer is instructed not to relate a privileged conversation to anyone, not even to his superiors, as was once suggested in a hearing of the New York legislature. Equally lacking in reassurance was the suggestion of the Justice Department, in 1962, that the agent in charge erase the privileged conversation from the tape before turning it over to anyone else.

Samuel Dash, in his book *The Eavesdroppers,* reported the understandable concern of a gambler: "It would be all right if it could be confined to cops catching criminals. But you get all kinds of talk—a guy has a sweetheart—or is abusing his wife . . . all that comes in. For this reason, I'm very much against it."

A wiretap placed on a suspect's telephone cannot make any distinctions at all. It monitors and records privileged conversations as well as the talk of family, friends, and mere acquaintances. Placed on a business telephone, its range may become even wider because many of the persons involved in the monitored conversations would probably have no connection with the suspect.

A tap on a private telephone is abusive enough, but what about a tap on a public telephone? This kind of thing is by no means rare. In 1953–54, the New York City police tapped more than 3,500 telephones and almost half of these were public.

An IRS agent admitted to the Senate Subcommittee on Administrative Practice and Procedure that taps were placed on public telephones in the Chicago headquarters of IRS. By this means, the conversations of any number of innocent persons, totally unrelated to an investigation, are overheard by the police.

Sometimes the telephone to be tapped is tied to a trunk line in a hotel or a large business establishment. When this happens, a whole army of innocents can fall into the snooper's net.

But no matter where a tap is placed, the sneak—whether public or private—is sure to overhear many conversations, even of the suspect, that in no way serve the public interest. A Senate hearing in 1940 produced the dismaying example of a New York police officer who, by means of a single tap, overheard conversations involving the following: the Juilliard School of Music, Brooklyn Law School, Consolidated Radio Artists, Western Union, the Mercantile National Bank, the Medical Bureau to Aid Spanish

Democracy, brokers, engineers, a dry cleaner, numerous bars, and—a little welcome irony here—a New York police precinct stationhouse. There is no guarantee that a wiretap will pick up anything of value to law enforcement. But what is almost certain is that the policeman manning the tap will overhear conversations that are none of his, or the government's, business.

A bug, like a wiretap, is undiscriminating in its coverage, but its sweep is different. A wiretap, tied into a telephone line, can spread its tentacles over the globe. The bug, on the other hand, works in depth. It picks up all conversation within its range over a prolonged period. Its sweep is not geographically broad, but many find it more potent and frightening than the tap. It, too, is not able to separate the different types of conversation it tunes in on—privileged, innocent, or relevant. It serves as a giant ear, taking in everything indiscriminately for the policeman to hear.

A case decided by the Supreme Court in 1954—*Irvine* vs. *California*—gives some idea of how gamey this kind of thing can be. Here, the Los Angeles police, by means of a surreptitiously installed microphone, monitored all the bedroom conversation of a suspected bookmaker and his wife over a long period of time.

The wiretaps and bugs mentioned so far were usually installed and monitored without the knowledge of those whose conversations were being overheard. But other techniques are available. Sometimes one of the parties to a conversation will know it is being recorded or that a third person is listening in. Law-enforcement officers will often record their own conversations with suspects or make arrangements for fellow officers to overhear such conversations. This is done not only to provide evidence but sometimes to protect the undercover agent himself.

Victims of crimes such as extortion, kidnaping, and bribery will often cooperate in acts of monitoring. Also, a hoodlum may, either voluntarily, for money, or through coercion, help the police to tune in on his chats with fellow criminals. When one of the parties knows of the monitoring, there is a species of control—the tap can be confined to conversations with certain persons. But the discrimination exercised may turn out to be no greater than in cases where the monitoring is unknown to all persons who use the tapped telephone.

When a wiretap or bug is installed without the knowledge of anyone whose conversation is to be overheard, there is a clear invasion of privacy. Even the most fervent advocates of law-enforcement wiretapping and bugging agree to this. In 1962, testifying in favor of wiretap legislation before a Senate committee, Attorney General Robert Kennedy said that, "In some respects, wiretapping involves a greater invasion of privacy than does a search."

The advocates of law-enforcement eavesdropping tend to believe that the use of these techniques has greater weight in the public interest than does the individual's right to privacy. But among these advocates there are many different points of view. Some hold that officers should have complete freedom to use such methods whenever they believe them helpful. Less extreme is the second view that there should be tight control within the law-enforcement agency. A third group believes the techniques should be used only when authorized by a court order.

As if these differences were not enough, there are separate opinions as to what crimes justify the use of wiretaps and bugs. Some argue for blanket availability, permitting such use in all crimes. Others want these methods employed only in specific crimes. The list of specific crimes varies widely, however, from person to person. Finally, there are different admixtures of all these separate positions.

An example of just how involved this kind of thinking can get is the wiretap bill sent to Congress by the Attorney General in 1962. If passed integrally, it would have allowed federal wiretapping on court order in crimes affecting national security, and in those involving murder, kidnaping, extortion, narcotics, bribery, transmission of gambling information, and travel or transportation in aid of racketeering enterprises. The bill would also have allowed federal wiretapping in cases affecting national security solely on the Attorney General's authorization. On the state level, wiretapping would have been permitted on court order where the crimes were murder, kidnaping, extortion, bribery, or dealing in narcotic drugs or marijuana. During the hearings on the bill, it was urged that the federal list be expanded to include counterfeiting and robbery, and the state list to include gambling, larceny, fraud, robbery, and burglary. How do you stop the ball once it starts rolling?

Wiretapping and bugging are undoubtedly helpful to the police in some instances. But experience indicates that their value is limited.

New York State authorizes the police to wiretap with court orders. Frank Hogan, District Attorney of New York County, has called wiretapping "the single most important weapon in the fight against organized crime," and he has said that without it "law enforcement in New York is virtually crippled in the area of organized crime." Yet, according to his own statistics covering the years of 1950–59, a period in which his office handled an average of 34,000 criminal cases each year, his office's use of wiretapping was confined to an average of twenty-two cases a year.

In 1953, Miles McDonald, District Attorney of Brooklyn, said, "You usually use it [wiretapping] at a time when there is a continuing crime, where there is a conspiracy, where there is underworld machinery in operation." He indicated that the technique was unlikely to be used with any frequency in other cases.

New York State Assemblyman Anthony P. Savarese, a vigorous proponent of law-enforcement wiretapping, gave further weight to this view: "All they [law-enforcement officers] want to do is to exercise surveillance over his [a known criminal's] phone. This is the whole purpose of law-enforcement tapping. If they know that a certain crime is going to be committed, there is no point in tapping his wire. It is to find out what this known criminal is going to do that you want the surveillance over his phone."

These three men spoke from years of experience, and they presented substantial evidence that electronic eavesdropping is generally useful in three situations only: (1) solution of continuing crimes such as gambling, prostitution, and extortion; (2) apprehension of fugitives by tapping the telephones of their families and friends; (3) general intelligence-gathering on the underworld. Mr. William Hundley, Chief of the Organized Crime Section of the Justice Department, referring to this same question, told a Senate subcommittee in 1966: "Particularly in the field of illegal gambling, it [wiretapping] would be helpful for local officials, but when you are dealing with the hard-core racketeers, they just don't say anything on the telephone, so it would not be particularly helpful in that field."

Many people oppose the use of these clandestine techniques for any reason, or in any form. They give great weight to the fact that these methods are not especially helpful in solving major crimes. They point out that it has never been proved that other law-enforcement methods are so inadequate as to make these snooping techniques indispensable. They insist that the primary purpose behind the use of these techniques is to make law enforcement *easier but not more effective* (see end of Chapter 1).

Justice Samuel Hofstadter, of New York, has issued wiretap orders under that state's law. In 1955, he pointed out that, "Some years ago I instituted the requirement . . . that written reports of the results obtained from any interception order be thereafter submitted to me. Even with these restrictions, I have granted the orders with reluctance. The reports received by me, instead of allaying my anxiety, merely deepened it. These showed some arrests and fewer convictions and then rarely, if ever, for a heinous offense." The judge went on to say, "The right of privacy is the right 'to be let alone'—the right of 'inviolate personality.' A tapped wire is the greatest invasion of privacy possible. However rationalized, its authorized use has its roots in the amoral doctrine that the end justifies the means." The judge's later comments give support to the major argument of the opponents of law-enforcement wiretapping and bugging: these techniques are offensive to liberty, they are unconstitutional, and they are completely contrary to the idea of a free society. The price we pay for their use is too high.

Much of the foregoing is applicable to private use of wiretapping and bugging, as well. This discussion has been centered on government use of these techniques for two reasons: first, intrusion by the government strikes far more fundamentally at the individual than does private snooping. The ability to protect oneself against a nonofficial snooper is greater, and there is, in addition, a better chance to recoup any loss. Second, the private use of these methods is universally condemned, and the issue is thus simplified. Few people would seriously try to justify private wiretapping and bugging. Even among private detectives, many are of the opinion that these techniques are proper only when the client is the direct subscriber to the telephone being tapped, or the owner or tenant of the premises being bugged. When wiretaps and bugs are used, they must meet with the approval of the private eye's client. Most persons who hire snoopers seem to feel that, while such activity is generally evil, it is justified in their particular case. As in so many situations where human beings are involved, self-interest may blur the moral sense.

As we know, physical searches and seizures, wiretaps and bugs, are not the only means of assault on the privacy of one's home and person. They are only two types of weapon in a whole arsenal of techniques that include mass arrest, the agent provocateur, the paid informer, the lie detector, the psychological test, the mail cover, the two-way mirror, the miniature TV camera, and the snooper-scope—to name just a few. All these means, both personal and mechanical, for engaging in moral blitzkrieg have been used by government agents in the United States. They are still available, along with many more, and they are subject to little if any legal control.

Every one of these techniques should be analyzed carefully to determine to what extent it invades the privacy each American has a right to enjoy. No thinking citizen will question the need to enforce our laws. But what should most certainly be questioned by every morally responsible American is the conventional plea that the methods discussed here are "necessary." As the younger William Pitt said, "Necessity is the argument of tyrants; it is the creed of slaves." And the memory of official necessity, as practiced in Nazi Germany and in other dictatorships, should be all too clear and frightening.

It is important to liberty that all Americans recognize and cherish the right of privacy. The task of safeguarding privacy and freedom remains where it has always been—with the people. They will get the privacy they are willing to demand and fight for, and not an inch or a moment more. This is what Judge Learned Hand was talking about when he said, "Liberty lies in the hearts of men and women; when it dies there, no constitution, no law, no court can save it; no constitution, no law, no court can even do much to help it."

3

You Are the Target

ELBOWROOM IS RAPIDLY DISAPPEARING in the United States. At our present rate of growth, the population will double by the year 2000, and a hundred years from now there will be nearly a billion of us. Right now, the presence of almost 200 million people within our boundaries is enough to raise many serious problems related to individual liberty. A man who does not want to share his thoughts and actions with other persons has to be more cautious than formerly about what he says or does, and where he says or does it.

In a country swarming with people, "togetherness" is not the only challenge to individual freedom. When cities grow large, they create threats to public health and safety. To protect the general welfare, most large communities have adopted health and safety codes, and appointed inspectors to enforce them. Such inspectors often have broad powers to enter and examine homes and buildings.

The Supreme Court has upheld the constitutionality of the power given to these public health and safety inspectors. A 1959 decision approved the right of a health inspector to demand entrance into a home without a warrant and without probable cause. Evidence of rat infestation outside the home was held to justify his demand for entry. A 1960 decision upheld a demand for entry by housing inspectors, even where they had no occasion to suspect any housing violation. It would seem clear from this that, for the city dweller at least, the sanctity of the home is no longer to be taken literally.

Our society is not only crowded but highly complex. This poses a special threat to individual freedom, because in such a society there are many who, for whatever reason, feel pressed to keep records. We are living in the age of the dossier. Never before in our history have such quantities of personal data been collected by so many different groups about so many people. The Cold War, crime, big business, big government, a credit economy, all these have contributed to the spread of this practice. And modern technology has helped it to boom.

Almost all business firms collect a certain amount of personal data on employees and prospective employees. Almost invariably, applicants are expected to fill out forms that may include questions on educational background, past employment, past residences, creditors, associations with organizations, and religious affiliations, as well as personal references. The nature and number of details required depend on the individual firm.

In addition to a routine form, many employers collect extensive dossiers on present and even possible future employees. Most business firms limit elaborate records to top management personnel, but others apparently feel the need to put all employees under the microscope. Prospective employees of a firm engaged in national-defense work are subject to thorough field investigations by federal agencies, especially if the positions they are to fill are at high levels. In order to avoid loss of time and money in the event that a job candidate does not receive clearance, some employers working on national-defense contracts have their own means of running intensive investigations of prospective employees. Until these are satisfactorily completed, the candidate will not be put to work even at acquainting himself with the nonclassified aspects of his new duties.

The exhaustive probe is by no means limited to firms with national-defense contracts. The dossier-minded employer can be found in every line of business. With many firms, from insurance companies to the oil industry, the collection of data has become an integral part of hiring and promotion. Often a private detective agency is employed to do the job. Its investigators check candidates thoroughly; their routine reports include examinations of academic records, court records, personal credit and litigation, marital status, police records, political affiliation, neighborhood background, newspaper files, past earning capacity and past employment records, personal (drinking and even sexual) habits and conduct, and moral character.

The concern of the employer may extend to the prospective employee's wife and family. If the position entails such public relations activities as entertaining or extensive social interchange, he will undoubtedly want to know about the prospective employee's wife, so a dossier is prepared on her, too. There will be a full report on her character and a compilation of her controversial characteristics, including her social mannerisms and drinking habits; reference will be made to her education and to her ability to adjust to her home and neighborhood; a list of her club and religious affiliations will be included. The president of the Burns Detective Agency has written that, "When the Agency undertakes investigations of this sort, the subject emerges as well known to his prospective employer as he is to his own family—in some cases better."

The field investigation is not the only method used to compile a dossier. After all, this method leaves the applicant with a few elements of personal information that the snoopers have not been able to obtain, so the employer may use the psychological test and the polygraph. This last is commonly, but erroneously, called the "lie-detector." Through the use of these techniques, the investigator can examine the prospective employee's modes of thinking. Questions of a most personal nature are often asked and the personality of the subject may be effectively revealed by the answers.

In 1964, Congressman Cornelius Gallagher told of a seventeen-year-old girl applying for a typing job, who was required to submit to a polygraph test, adding, "This girl was asked many questions concerning not only her personal and social life but her sex life. She was subjected to questions that were most embarrassing and she suffered a humiliating experience."

In a similar case reported to a Senate subcommittee hearing a year later, the girl job applicant had had to take a psychological test. Among the "true" and "false" statements she had been asked to check were: "Many of my dreams are about sex matters." "Once in a while I think of things too bad to talk about." "I feel sure there is only one true religion." "I like to listen to or tell jokes in which sex plays a major part." "I like to read books and plays in which sex plays a major part."

Such questioning techniques tend to reveal more about the employee than he may know himself, and more than any prospective employer has the right to know.

The zeal of the private employer for collecting personal information about a job applicant is matched by that of the federal government. Although a single personal-data form (Form 57) must be filled out in applying for Civil Service employment, individual federal agencies that hire from the Civil Service rolls may have more than one form of their own.

In addition to field investigations required by most government agencies, several of them make use of the psychological tests and the polygraph. The more security-sensitive agencies, such as the CIA and the National Security Agency, use them regularly. The FBI also checks its files for other government agencies, and any indication of disloyalty unleashes an added investigation by the Bureau.

It should be noted that, whether or not the individual obtains the position in private industry or in government service for which he has applied, all the personal data in his dossier remain in the hands of strangers. Some of these strangers may, of course, be private detectives.

In the compilation of a field report, one source of information on an applicant that is almost always checked is the Credit Bureau. Since few of us have failed to use credit at some time, this organization has information on most adult Americans. It is meant primarily to serve the needs of local businesses, but its information is often readily available to anyone willing to pay for preparation of a report.

The practiced snooper also knows that a search of the records kept in the average county courthouse will provide him with many leads. Another source of detailed personal information is the insurance company, whose representatives must make responsible judgments in the issuance of its policies.

In some ways, the professional researcher is even more thorough than the hired snooper. He is a record collector whose activities have expanded rapidly in recent years. From the Gallup pollster to the university sociologist, the researcher collects information on individual habits, views, and behavior. Here again, the information may be for a specific and reasonable purpose, but there is always the potential for unjustifiable invasion of privacy.

The government is, of course, the greatest single collector of information about the individual. Aside from the questions of the Census Bureau, there are those of the Internal Revenue Service. The IRS maintains a vast reservoir of facts and figures about the average person's private affairs.

Most Americans do not object to sharing with the IRS the private details of their economic status. They have the impression that their tax returns are confidential and that the information they contain will be used for tax purposes only. But in life this inviolability is a dream: tax returns are subject to inspection by all departments and agencies of the federal government and the Congress. They are also subject to inspection by state and local governments. The procedures for obtaining access to tax returns may vary, *but they are available.*

The FBI is an assiduous collector of information about people, and even such routine papers as a draft card, a social security card, or army discharge forms represent separate collections of personal data about individuals.

In recent years, the accumulation of almost unmanageable records has given rise to special problems. But electronic data-processing has solved many of these problems. Information can now be fed into a machine as collected, and the full data sheet on any individual can be retrieved in a matter of seconds. Government and private industry are rapidly expanding their use of such equipment, and there are plans under way for a grand National Data Center where all government-held information will be stored in one computer.

A recent incident in New York indicates one of the more interesting uses of computers. A computer that had been fed accumulated information from bettors, police, and other sources spewed out the names of eighty-six alleged bookmakers. Indictments followed. The machine had not only stored the information but had evaluated it. The government claimed that this mechanical evaluation was necessary for, otherwise, the three-year statute of limitations on the charges might have expired before human investigators could have evaluated the data.

Commenting on the impact of computer-derived data in criminal cases, one lawyer said, "It [the computer] can tell you where the stars are going to be a million years from now. Do you think a jury is not going to believe that it can

1

2

3

Sen. Long (above) raises desk calendar to reveal microphone for eavesdropping. At the right (top), an FM transmitter that fits handily into a cigarette box; a bugged olive (center) with a swizzle-stick antenna for the end-of-day martini; and a dime-size mike.

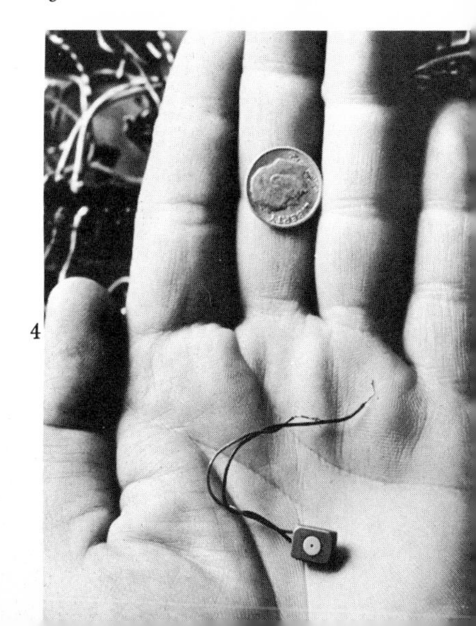
4

5

6

7

A telescopic lens lets a professional snooper take a photo (upper left) of someone passing premises under his surveillance from a quarter of a mile away; a special shotgun (lower left) has just released "spike mike" that, once imbedded in the frame of a window or door, transmits private conversations to the eavesdropper; the young man above, with solitary cup of coffee and room-service radio, is busy taping the conversation taking place at the party across a hotel court some fifty feet from him.

8

9

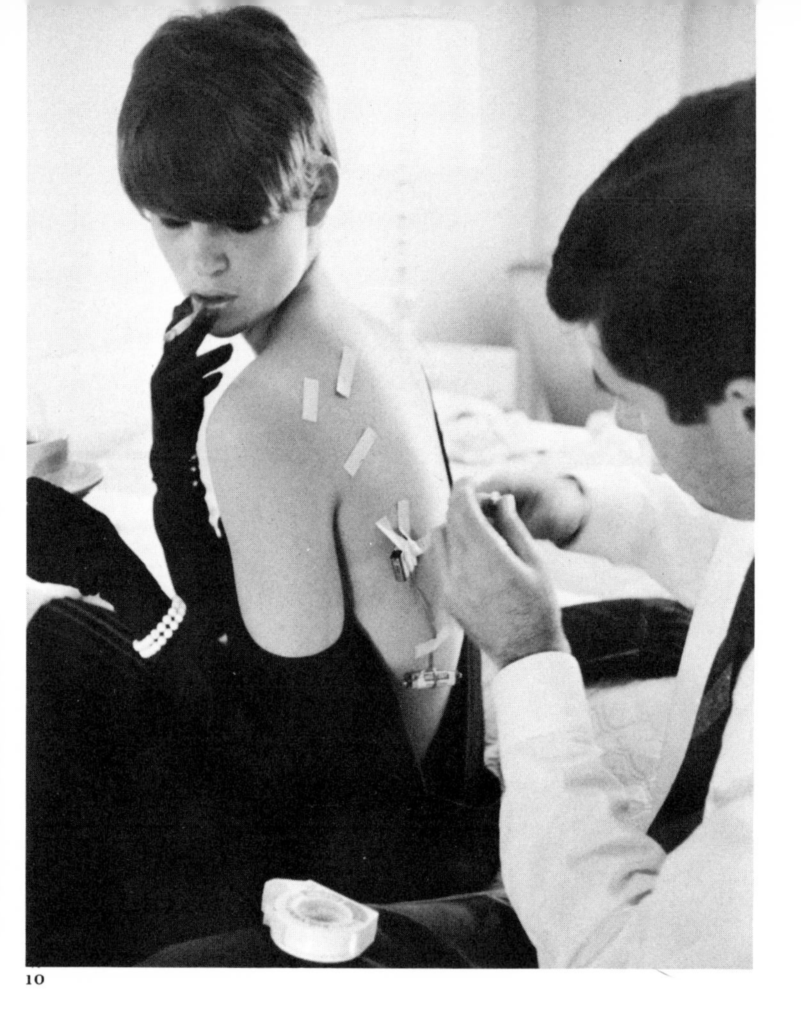

Pen at upper left points to "knot" in a wood picture frame concealing a transmitter that can operate for 200 hours on its own built-in battery. Below (left), the raised back of the picture exposes the hidden mechanism that includes a recording device. Above, the young woman watches as a "shocker" is attached to her skin and dimes are then taped above it to serve as electrodes. Her partner can now communicate coded shocks across a room to guide the wearer's actions, as in a game of cards, for example, in which transmission of information could be very important.

11

12

The production of electronic devices employs thousands and has become a multimillion dollar industry. The factory bench and workers shown at upper left are protected in turn from snoopers by an automatic camera, such as those used by banks to deter and identify robbers. The well-stocked counter and shelves (lower left) of this eavesdroppers' bazaar supplies official, i.e., government employed, tappers with the tools of their trade. But the shop caters to the unofficial snooper too. Anyone with $500 can buy such a miniature masterpiece as the plastic olive transmitter and toothpick antenna; for $250, there is a device that converts a victim's phone into a long-distance transmitter. Above, Jack Harwood, Palm Beach "private eye and ear extraordinary," poses amid electronic gadgets with which, in divorce cases alone, he does a thriving business.

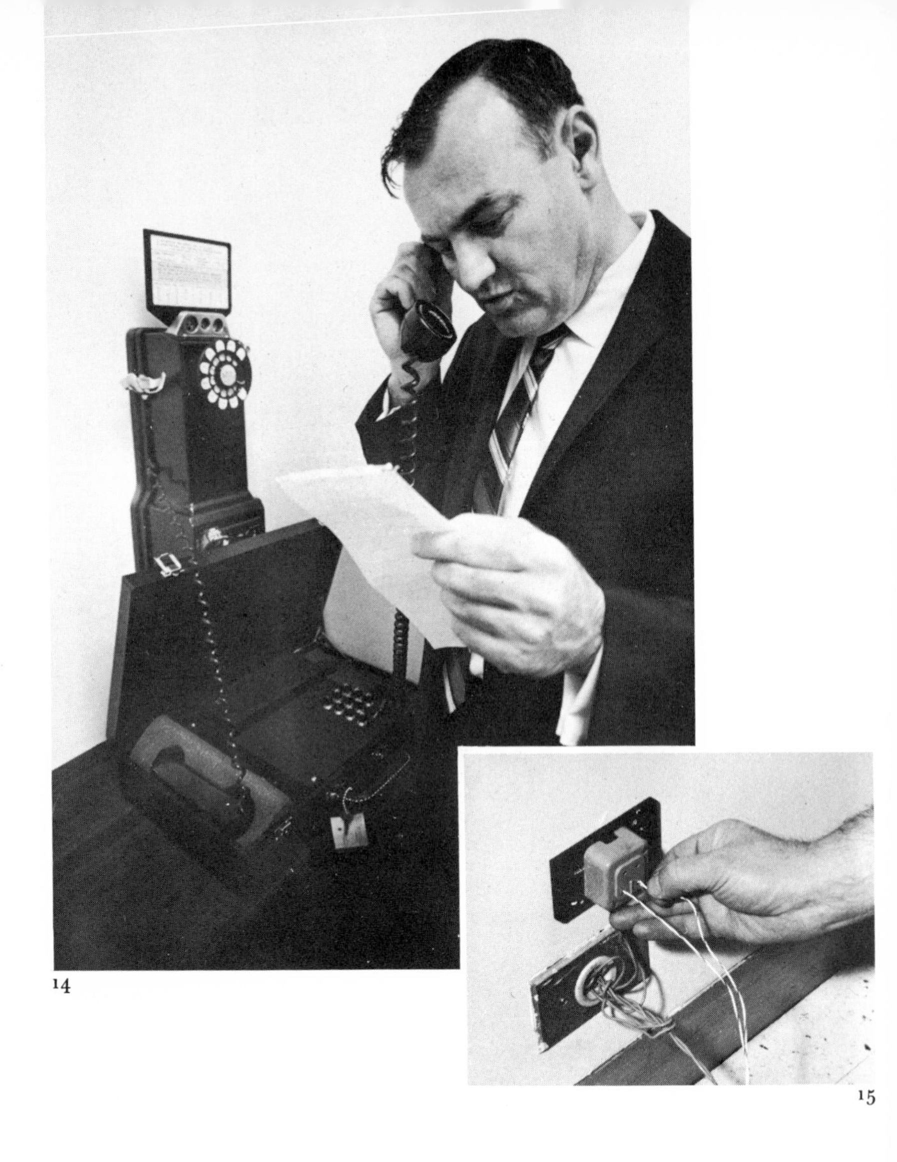

14

15

Victims of wiretaps believed until recently that pay phones were harder and less likely to be bugged than private wires. Above, an agent tapes a conversation from a pay phone. Below, the insertion of an additional wire transforms the home telephone into an amplifier and transmitter so that a snooper outside the home can record talk at his convenience.

tell you where a bookie is in the Bronx? It's just too sacrosanct and that's what scares me." In other words, it may someday be possible to manufacture a jury's verdict by machine.

Because of this diligent accumulation of facts about each of us, it is difficult to speak or act today without wondering if the words or actions will reappear "on the record." And the lack of spontaneity such a situation is bound to create will get worse. Unless there is a change in direction, the time is coming—it may already be here for some—when the average person will have to pause to consider the implications of every spoken word and every action in view of its possible interpretation. Spontaneous activity, always the special hallmark of a democracy, is in the process of being stamped out.

Record keeping and push-button fact-finding are only part of the pressure being put on individual freedom. In many other ways, restraints visible and not so visible are placed on freedom of choice, freedom of action, and privacy itself.

In our affluent society, the consumer waits, dollar in hand, for the new and better products that may come along. Every medium of communication is used to persuade him that he not only needs a particular product but that something must be wrong with him if he does not already have it. Madison Avenue strives for conformity, because conformity of tastes and interests alone allows mass production to flourish and be profitable. The role of advertising in all this is primary, and in recent years ever more cunning forms of verbal seduction have been developed.

For example, the automatic telephone solicitor is a device that takes a long list of telephone numbers, calls them, plays a taped message, says good-bye, and hangs up. If the line is busy, or there is no answer, the device will call again later. One version of this instrument is not very polite. If the called party hangs up, the device will repeat the call, and continue to do so until the whole message is delivered. While all this is going on, it denies the person called the use of his own telephone. There are probably few modern inventions that have done so much as this one to produce a sense of futile outrage.

Another gift of technology to merchandising is the hidden camera which determines consumer reaction to products. When installed in a supermarket, this device records the shopper's reaction to particular displays or products. Without realizing it, many of us are taking screen tests these days. In the same place, of course, there is likely to be a two-way mirror to check on shoplifters, and a hidden camera to protect the store against writers of bad checks.

Vice Admiral Hyman Rickover, in October, 1965, warned that technology could become "a Frankenstein destroying its creator." He pointed out that science is the search for knowledge, while technology is the application of some part of that knowledge. He gave examples of man's shortsightedness in trying to gain immediate profit from such technology without thought to the consequences, and he referred to new techniques that "involve snooping into the inner recesses of the human mind, personality testing, and pseudo-scientific manipulation of human beings."

The Admiral made it clear that a technology directed to serve human needs will serve democratic institutions. But he warned that if technological advance is looked upon as a force that must be given its head, without sensible controls, then it will not only undermine democratic institutions but may well destroy us all.

This points a finger at the spread of the fantastic snooping devices recently developed—and which continue to be improved. Many people do not seem disturbed by the extent to which they can now infringe on the traditional American concept of individual liberty. The emphasis has been reversed, and these people find themselves trying to accommodate society and the Constitution to the use of the devices. Freedom to use the device rather than the freedom of the individual has become the basic issue.

In his farewell address to the American People, on January 17, 1961, President Eisenhower sounded a warning concerning our present situation: "This conjunction of an immense military establishment and a large arms industry is new in the American experience. The total influence—economic, political, even spiritual—is felt in every city, every State house, every office of the Federal government. We recognize the imperative need for this development. Yet we must not fail to comprehend its grave implications. Our toil, resources, and livelihood are all involved; so is the very structure of our society." President Eisenhower went on to warn that "we must guard against the acquisition of unwarranted influence, whether sought or unsought, by the military-industrial complex. . . . We must never let the weight of this combination endanger our liberties or democratic processes."

Communism has presented us not only with an external danger to our security but with an internal one as well. Of course, our nation must be protected from Communist espionage, sabotage, and subversion. Yet the difficulty of identifying the enemy creates its own internal dangers, too. During the McCarthy years, we went through a trying, almost an hysterical, experience in which neighbors eyed each other with grave suspicion. Hostility and fear were the order of the day, and even national leaders, including former President Truman, were charged with being irresponsible, fellow travelers, Communists, or tools of Communism.

McCarthyism and the appeal to fear and suspicion are still a part of the American scene. Right-wing organizations are busy proclaiming that our government, churches, and schools are infiltrated by Communists. The Supreme Court, and particularly the Chief Justice, are regularly accused of being dupes of the Kremlin. Fortunately, however, reason is more firmly in the saddle today than it was some fifteen years ago. Even so, where Communism is involved, the government tends to continue making exceptions in the protection of individual rights. One example is the Abel espionage case, already mentioned, in which the Supreme Court went to considerable lengths to justify the search of the suspect's room and belongings.

Another conspiracy against America's welfare, this one indigenous, is organized crime. Attorney General Nicholas Katzenbach said that it represents money, power, and terror. In his estimate, "illegal gambling alone totals on the order of seven billion dollars a year. And that says nothing about extortion, bribes, pay-offs, narcotics, loan-sharking, prostitution, business fraud, 'fire-for-hire' arson, and the other . . . rackets."

The federal government began its all-out war on organized crime shortly after Senator Kefauver's committee hearings on the situation in the early 1950's. This federal program was given new impetus by the revelation of the underworld's cabinet meeting at Appalachin in 1957. In 1961, Attorney General Robert Kennedy put still greater power behind the federal effort, and set up what is known as the Organized Crime Drive. He also persuaded Congress to enact new measures to help control interstate criminal movements.

The Organized Crime Drive involves the efforts of more than twenty-six separate federal law-enforcement agencies, and this has produced a new law-enforcement policy at the top. There has always been concern over the possible establishment of a national police force, inherently a threat to liberty. In the past, because of this concern, federal machinery would go into action only after a crime had been committed. But the Organized Crime Drive has brought a reversal in this traditional procedure. Once a suspected racket leader is identified, the federal agencies now try to establish his involvement in organized crime. This new policy brings us perilously close to a national police force. The Attorney General claims the new approach—with its network of interlocking federal agencies—is essential to fight organized crime, and it probably is. But it would be relatively easy for a future Attorney General to change the target from underworld leaders to some other group of

Americans he would like to get. Already, there are instances where the OCD mantle has been stretched rather far by agents to justify snooping into the lives of particular individuals, or to explain away the use of some eyebrow-raising investigative technique.

The OCD program, because of its size, its vigor, and the new law-enforcement policy which implements it, has brought considerable pressure to bear on individual rights. But beyond this threat from above, the public has, because of its concern with crime, put its own pressures on individual rights. The average man is usually more concerned with street crimes than with organized crime, and he knows that the reported crime rate has doubled in the past twenty-five years. The resulting pervasive fear has given rise to loud demands from the public for law enforcement at any cost. This has tended to submerge the individual's concern for his own rights and liberties. Throughout history, the combination of government zeal and public emotion has been responsible for the severest curtailment of individual freedom.

Government at all levels has grown rapidly over the past thirty years. This expansion has not come without certain costs to the individual. Few economic or personal decisions can be made today without consideration being given to some federal law.

At present there are more than 30,000 federal investigators, most of them dedicated men whose records are exemplary. But some of these men, unaware that they are servants of the people, have intimidated, threatened, and harassed individuals and groups. Some have used police-state techniques. Bureaucracy is inherent in big government, and such trespasses are not easy to correct. In the quagmire of red tape and official procedures, the significance of the individual's rights tends to sink, often without a trace.

Excessive pressures are already here in abundance and, unless they are recognized and stopped, we may slip past the point of no return. Over twenty-five years of hot and cold wars have dulled our sensitivities to individual freedom. So-called security has become an overriding concern to many Americans. It does not occur to many people that the men who drafted the Bill of Rights were quite familiar with espionage, sabotage, subversion, murder, mayhem, larceny, and robbery. Yet they chose the freedom guaranteed by the Fourth Amendment and the other provisions of our Constitution. These men could have had security as a colony of Britain, but they chose freedom. In the words of Jefferson, "Timid men . . . prefer the calm of despotism to the boisterous seas of liberty."

Most of these excessive pressures have established themselves gradually. Affluence and the passion for "security" have smoothed the way for their acceptance. Reports of them, when publicized, too rarely cause general concern. Today, parents smile as they buy toys in the form of electronic snooping gear designed especially for children. And research studies indicate that, on the adult level, several provisions of the Bill of Rights would not find easy acceptance if put to a national referendum.

Modern technology will soon make mechanically practical the nightmare society projected by George Orwell in *1984*. If we are to avoid such a fate, we must begin to take the actions necessary to protect the sanctity of the home and the inviolability of the person. Inspection of the home without a warrant, the compilation of dossiers, the use of electronic snooping and of such "brain-watching" devices as the polygraph, and psychological testing must all be carefully considered. If these practices are adjudged acceptable, to what extent and under what circumstances should they be allowed? And who should be allowed to use them? In seeking to answer these questions, we must first provide an atmosphere in which human personality can develop, experiment and creativity can flourish, ideas can be exchanged freely and fully, and personal relationships can grow without suspicion.

The foregoing gives only a limited review of the nearly overwhelming forces with which modern society confronts us, forces that tend to destroy privacy, and stultify imagination, initiative, and creativity; forces that serve to cast all men in the same mold. Many of these forces are here to stay, and we will have to learn to live with them. But this does not mean that we should allow ourselves to surrender our individual personalities. There is no reason why conformity must be made an inescapable part of the American dream. Excessive pressures can and must be prevented: there must be preserved in each individual a sphere of privacy that will allow his personality to bloom and thrive.

Judge Learned Hand, in a 1952 address, provided for many Americans an answer not only to McCarthyism but also to the current pursuit of the most intimate personal facts:

I believe that community is already in process of dissolution where each man begins to eye his neighbor as a possible enemy, where non-conformity with the accepted creed, political as well as religious, is a mark of disaffection; where denunciation, without specification or backing, takes the place of evidence; where orthodoxy chokes freedom of dissent; where faith in the eventual supremacy of reason has become so timid that we dare not enter our convictions in the open lists to win or lose. Such fears . . . may in the end subject us to despotism as evil as any that we dread; and they can be allayed only insofar as we refuse to proceed on suspicion, and trust one another until we have tangible ground for misgiving. . . .

The time for action is now.

4

The Eavesdropper's Arsenal

At the present time, there are methods and techniques available to observe and overhear a person's every act and word wherever he may be. *In the developmental stage are techniques to determine what a person is thinking and to control his thought.* Certain elementary techniques of this kind are already in use. To understand the scope of currently available threats to privacy, it is necessary to look in some detail at the arsenal of today's snooping equipment.

Many eavesdroppers, both governmental and private, are electronics experts, or work closely with such experts, and their tools and techniques are often custom-made. Information about these devices is carefully controlled and is usually revealed only by accident.

It was learned in the Kansas City hearings of the Senate Subcommittee on Administrative Practice and Procedure that the FBI had taken a composition plate which is a standard part of the telephone apparatus and had built an apparently identical part containing a tiny microphone.

The FBI then, by means of leased lines, had monitored from its own office all conversations in the room in which the device had been installed. The use of these devices was subsequently brought to light in other parts of the country as well.

The great majority of eavesdropping, however, is not done with such custom-built devices but with equipment of standard manufacture, or with home-made tools of a standard nature. Today this is a multi-million-dollar business. One New York firm specializing in over-the-counter snooping equipment announced, in the fall of 1965, the opening of its fifth retail outlet, and it also promised that it would soon be opening ten more stores. The firm got its start only three years before this announcement. It would be unwise to assume that so-called standard or over-the-counter equipment is lacking in technical sophistication.

Until a few years ago, the telephone tap was the principal method of electronic snooping in this country, but improvements in bugging devices have brought the bug into almost as high repute among experienced snoopers. Still, the wiretap holds the lead. There are three basic methods for tapping a telephone: the direct tap, the indirect or induction-coil tap, and the microphone tap.

Agreement is general that when a direct tap is properly installed, only the most careful physical search of the telephone line can possibly locate it. And even then it cannot always be detected. In testimony before a House subcommittee in 1955, an electronics expert boasted that he could install a tap based on a technique that had remained undetected through more than two dozen inspections. He also told of a tap that would destroy itself if someone either deliberately, or by accident, came too close for comfort. After destruction, there would be no evidence that it had ever existed.

The indirect or induction-coil method does not require any connection to the telephone line. It is only necessary to insert such a coil in the magnetic field created by the current on a telephone line. It is normally most effective to find a place where the two wires of the line are separated, and place the coil nearby. The expert who boasted of his undetectable taps expressed the professional view that the skillful tapper shies from the induction method and is likely to resort to it only if the direct tap will not serve his purpose.

Access to the line is generally essential for a satisfactory induction-coil tap, but the House subcommittee was told that an induction coil can, with certain auxiliary equipment, pick up conversations on a telephone line at a distance of fifty feet. In addition, this particular equipment is so discriminating that it can monitor the conversation over one telephone in a bank of telephone booths.

The third method, the microphone tap, requires access to the telephone itself. A small microphone is concealed inside it or sufficiently close to it to overhear both ends of the conversation. Despite its obvious limitations, this method has increased in popularity in recent years.

Not long ago, the wiretapper might have to sit for days in a cold basement or in a dusty attic, earphones to his head, transcribing by hand the conversations he overheard. If it was a police tap, a squad of men might be engaged to cover the tap in shifts. Today, a tap can be monitored by one man with little inconvenience. He need only stop by the listening post or "plant" every so often to change the reels on his tape or wire recorder. The new automatic equipment not only provides verbatim transcripts but, to conserve tapes, it "listens" and records only when voices are actually on the line.

Originally, the wiretapper used only wires. Then a conductive paint was developed. This paint comes in all colors, and will carry current just as a wire does. By the application of a strip of paint an undetectable circuit can be run along a wall.

Tappers have been particularly heartened by improvements in radio transmitters. Today, small transmitters are often used as at least part of the relay between the tap and the plant. This increases speed of installation and removal of taps, makes for flexibility in locating plants, and decreases the chances that the tapper will be found even if the tap should be discovered. Also, the place where the transmitter is located may increase chances that the tap itself will remain undetected.

In one publicized instance, IRS agents tapped three telephone lines by wiring a transmitter to each, right at the telephone pole. The receiver and recorder were set up in the home of an IRS supervisor, insuring maximum comfort for the tax collectors.

Many devices are available that permit a telephone conversation to be monitored with the knowledge of one party to the call, and certain of these work in conjunction with telephone extensions. Some snoopers contend that this practice of listening in on an extension is not actually wiretapping, but the person who does not know of the third ear usually has another opinion.

In addition to the wiretap, the snooper has three basic tools: the bug, the transmitter, and the recorder. The bug is a concealed or disguised microphone wired into a room to overhear conversation. The transmitter is a combination of a miniature microphone and transmitter, which may be hidden in a room or carried concealed on the person. The recorder is a combination microphone-recorder which can be concealed on the body or in a brief case. The snooper who uses these tools may go about his work, secure in the knowledge that his actions are virtually undetectable.

If he has access to the area to be monitored, the snooper will use one type of equipment, if not, he has recourse to another. He may, of course, obtain access by breaking and entering, or by subterfuge, but such acts are worse than illegal or immoral in his eyes: they increase his chances of being discovered.

Having gained access, the snooper has all kinds of opportunities, thanks to the telephone. Not only can it be tapped to monitor telephone conversations, but it provides ready-made microphones for monitoring room conversations, a power source for listening devices, and wiring to carry purloined conversations outside the room.

Because of its great potential, the telephone is always checked thoroughly when snooping is suspected. In fact, many security-minded people will never discuss confidential matters in a room where there is a telephone.

The lack of a telephone does not impede the practiced snooper, however. He may even avoid using one that is available because he knows that it is the first item checked in a search for listening devices. He may prefer to use a concealed bug or microphone. In addition to the telephone, he is likely to find other adaptable equipment awaiting his use.

In a hotel room, the Muzak system may be adapted so that the room speaker serves as a microphone. In an apartment building, the door signal system may provide a similar opportunity, except that a mike will then have to be hidden somewhere inside the apartment. Many schools, businesses, and even homes use an intercom. If the snooper has access to the control board, he, too, can make use of the system without any modifications. (Such systems are frequently used by supervisory personnel to check on employees. School principals have been publicized for using intercom systems to monitor both teachers and students. . . . "Big Brother *is* listening to you!")

The microphone used by a snooper may be the size of a postage stamp or even smaller. It may be hidden in a lamp, a closet, under a rug, or anywhere that wiring can be concealed. Instead of wires, the snooper may decide to use a transmitter, and he can buy one today that is no larger than an aspirin tablet. It may operate by batteries, in which case its life is limited, or be plugged into the house current where it may operate as long as the householder continues to pay his electric bills. In a Senate hearing, it was revealed that one such installation was used for eighteen months. When retrieved, the transmitter was still operating perfectly.

Battery-powered transmitters can be concealed almost anywhere, and the smaller they are the easier their concealment. One transmitter demonstrated before the same

Senate committee was hidden in a rose. Another possible hiding place is the dirt surrounding a potted plant.

On the snooping frontier, research marches on. A recent device is the microcircuit, made up of layers of metal 1/1000th of an inch thick sandwiched together. It draws its power from radio waves in the air and, as long as a commercial radio station in the vicinity is on the air, it will transmit. This transmitter is so small that it may be concealed in a slit in the side of a playing card or placed inside wallpaper.

A technique similar to the transmitter is commonly referred to as the microwave. In this case, a microphone and a reflecting device like a transmitter are hidden in a room. From a point outside the room, a microwave beam is directed at the device which reflects it, the reflection carrying the room conversation. The reflected beam is then picked up by a receiver. This method is one of the most difficult to detect, but it remains, fortunately, beyond the means of the average snooper. The Russians used it to bug the U.S. Embassy in Moscow.

Many large hotels across the country are believed to have permanently bugged rooms. According to reports, certain guests are assigned to these rooms, at the request of law-enforcement officials. Some people will probably be grateful for this kind of corporate thoughtfulness, since it relieves government agents of the need to install anything so undignified as a bug. Others may be less appreciative.

It should not be assumed that the potential victim has no need for concern if the snooper is somehow prevented from gaining access to the target home or office. The list of devices and techniques available for use *without* access is as long as it is versatile. *Because lack of access is more common than access, most of the research on snooping techniques is aimed at the development of techniques that meet this need.*

The telephone remains a major ally of the snooper, even when he lacks direct access to it. A recently developed device, when attached to a line at any terminal box, will promptly turn the telephone into a permanent microphone. This sinister adapter is commonly known as the "black box." It can activate the telephonic microphone even though the handpiece is in the cradle. All room conversations, in addition to phone conversations, can then be monitored. Because it uses high radio frequency current, this technique is very difficult to detect. This device is not yet available to the ordinary eavesdropper, but it probably will be soon.

To attach this device or a conventional wiretap, the snooper must locate the proper telephone line at a place where the necessary connections can be made. An alert snooper is sometimes able to obtain the information he needs simply by calling the telephone office and posing as a telephone repairman. Or, if the tapper is a law-enforcement officer, he may be able to secure the outright cooperation of the telephone company in the placing of his taps. In Kansas City, the existence of just such an arrangement between the telephone company and the chief of police was revealed.

Bugs and transmitters, as well as wiretaps, are important tools of the snooper who lacks access to the target area. If the room to be monitored is in an apartment, office building, or hotel, the investigator can rent the room next door; he can then place a contact mike *on* a connecting door; he can place a keyhole extension mike *in* the door; or he can slide a small mike *under* the door. This last technique was used in the Goldfine case of 1958, but the snooper stuck the mike so far under the door that it was exposed on the other side. Also ready to hand for the pryer are a wall detector, an electronic stethoscope, and a spike mike. This last is a tiny microphone on the back of a long spike. The spike is inserted in the wall until the point comes in contact with the other wall. In this way, the victim's wall becomes a large sounding board.

If the snooper rents the room above his victim, he can lower a mike down an air duct or out the window. In some situations, he may gain access to false ceilings, attics or basements that provide opportunities to monitor the target area. In a recent New Hampshire case, a microphone was found monitoring the bedroom conversation of a husband and wife who had rented a house. The landlord, who had water pumps operating in the basement, claimed that the mike was for the purpose of monitoring his pumps. Judgment in the case was in favor of the landlord-defendant.

In a Louisiana case, it was alleged that the victim had been given a stuffed animal inside which was a small transmitter. This technique obviously requires that the snooper know the victim well enough to justify a gift. Also, if the snooper can intercept furniture, lamps, or other objects being delivered to the victim's home or office, he can place transmitters in them.

The brief-case recorder is, of course, useful. Posing as a salesman, interviewer, or business client, the snooper can leave his brief-case recorder behind. Subsequently, he can return to retrieve the property he has "forgotten."

So far, all techniques except the wiretap have required if not access to the target room then at least to the building in which the room is located. There are, however, a number of devices and techniques that can be used entirely from outside. A microphone may be hidden just outside a window, if the window is open. If the building is multistoried, the snooper may turn to the telescopic or parabolic microphone. This device, which is also used by TV reporters to cover news events and football games, will pick up the conversation of persons five hundred feet away and will block out all side talk. If the snooper can find a spot in a nearby building, or other cover, from which he can aim this device into the open window of the victim, he can obtain gratifying results.

The snooper may place a small contact mike on the pane of a closed window, or he may drive a spike mike into the window frame, with the point just touching the pane. In some cases, this same type of mike can also be driven into the outside wall.

New and more insidious techniques for monitoring rooms without physically entering them are making their appearance on the market. Most are still in the developmental stage, but some are already available. These techniques include the use of infrared light beams, laser beams, and sonic spectrums. The infrared and laser techniques hold a potential for monitoring not only what is said but what is done behind closed doors. Both sound and picture would be reflected from the target area. Technology has only begun to develop the capabilities of these techniques, but even this beginning should be enough to alarm the customary target of such cunning: the general public.

The snooper may easily pursue his interests on the street, in automobiles, and in public places like bars or restaurants. On the street, he may monitor with a telescopic mike and by use of concealed recorders and transmitters on one of the talkers. A small recorder can be carried conveniently in a shoulder holster, and a transmitter the size of a pack of cigarettes will, when carried in the pocket, raise no suspicions. The microphone for either of these devices can be concealed in a tie clip, a button, a wrist watch, or a fountain pen.

There are reports of a transmitter so small that it can fit under a fingernail, but the one the size of a cigarette package is likely to give more satisfactory results. When a transmitter is sending from an automobile, it may be necessary for the snooper to follow in his own car in order to keep the receiver within range. To facilitate tailing, there are devices that can be installed underneath a victim's car which then proceed to emit signals. The latest tailing equipment also informs the listener of the general direction in which the tailed car is going.

Some transmitters not yet used for snooping promise distinct advantages. Among these are a transmitter-receiver combination that will fit in a human ear, a transmitter that can be installed inside a hollow tooth, and transmitters that have been placed in the stomachs of animals, through ingestion of food. These latter transmitters draw their current from the body of the animal.

A Chinese proverb tells us that one picture is worth a thousand words. Technology has provided marvels in the photographic area, too. Concealable movie and still cameras are available that are completely automatic, that can be operated by remote control, and that are so sensitive to the presence of human beings that they take pictures only when people are near. Closed-circuit TV cameras have been reduced in size until today there is a camera smaller than an ordinary flashlight. It can easily be concealed in air ducts or lighting fixtures. Infrared light or electronic light simplifiers can be used to take pictures even in the dark. Not many years ago, one of our officials in the U.S. Embassy in Warsaw was caught passing information to the Communists: our security agents had recorded certain of his nocturnal activities with this kind of equipment.

But sound and film are not the end of the story, either. Aside from the already mentioned lie detector and the psychological test, there are truth serums and other useful drugs. Scientists have long been able to reproduce brain waves on graphs, and work is now under way to translate these tracings to actual thought patterns. Success here will put modern snooping technology even ahead of Hitler: in Nazi Germany the mind was safe, at least while it was asleep.

People who have lived in a police state have discovered reasonably simple ways to foil the snooper. Cover can be provided by turning up the volume of the radio or TV set, and talking close together very quietly. In the home, the sound of the shower will drown out normal conversation. A movie theater is a good place to discuss confidential matters, although a subway platform or moving train is even better. The purpose of all of these backdrops is to submerge the conversation in loud background noise.

If snooping is suspected, it is always helpful to be able to disconnect both the telephone and the electric current, but this is not always feasible. In such circumstances, an expert countersnooper could use a jammer or a loop antenna to discourage the eavesdropper.

It is not easy, even for a professional, to discover a microphone concealed in a room, and a wiretap can be even harder to find. Over the years, several devices for detecting wiretaps have been placed on the market, but wiretappers everywhere have been able to sleep soundly in the knowledge that none of these has been completely effective. There seems to be universal agreement that only a physical check of the line at every possible point between the instrument and the main frame, is likely to detect a tap. And not even then are results guaranteed. While little can be done to detect a tap, there are a number of techniques which purport to protect phone conversations against the tapper—most of them expensive and even impractical. One requires the use of a special neon tube. Another is the voice scrambler, which garbles conversation passing through the line.

The telephone companies realize the importance of privacy, and most, if not all, of them would like to provide a secure system. They use a variety of procedures to maintain the secrecy of communications but, despite this commendable caution, the system breaks down. When a wiretapper or his tap is discovered, the telephone company concerned generally seems too polite to seek prosecution. The tap may be reported to the police, but seldom will an official complaint be filed. If company employees are directly involved, they will probably be dismissed, but that is likely to be the end of it.

It would seem, therefore, that the telephone companies

are more concerned for the apparent than the actual security of the system. An example of this is the New York City wiretap operation discovered in 1955, in which two telephone company employees were found to be collaborating with a private investigator in the placing of taps. They were discharged, but the company did not press charges. This see-no-evil attitude of the telephone companies tarnishes the image of their conscientious efforts to make the system secure.

For many years, the tools of the eavesdropper were the exclusive property of the professionals. While anyone could go into a neighborhood radio shop and buy components for a listening device, he was not apt to do so. If he wanted information that could only be obtained through electronic snooping, he employed a private detective. Today, he can also try his own hand at snooping.

Several of our leading newspapers and magazines advertise snooping gear, according to which the products seem suitable not only for the professional but also for those who are merely curious. The equipment offered for sale runs from $3 induction coils to complete security kits at $349. One ad in a major daily newspaper offered an attaché case with a built-in, concealed, ultra-sensitive microphone, a telephone pick-up adapter that trips the recorder when a telephone call is started, a wireless transmitter that may be carried in a shirt pocket, a tie clip or cuff link microphone, a new keyhole extension mike that many would find indispensable, and a number of other ingenious items calculated to turn us all into a nation of Peeping Toms overnight.

Another recent ad in a national magazine has offered for

sale, at less than $20, a parabolic microphone which could keep the listener informed of what people were talking about five hundred feet away. Such devices may be purchased by mail or across the counter in most major cities, and if the buyer has the price, he is rarely asked any embarrassing questions.

Several years ago, Justice William O. Douglas wrote, in his book *The Rights of the People,* "The truth is that wiretapping today is a plague on the nation. . . . Now all the intimacies of one's private life can be recorded. This is far worse than ransacking one's desk and closets. This is a practice that strikes as deep as an invasion of the confessional."

The human quest for knowledge is one thing; the rapacious quest for ordinarily private information is quite another.

5

"Insidious encroachments by men of zeal . . ."

CONSIDERING THE ARMY of well-equipped snoopers moving about the country today, and the general public's concern over crime and national security, it might help to review the history of the federal government's use of wiretapping. It is marked by evidence of excesses on the part of federal officers who have trampled over individual privacy and rights.

Some facts come from court records, Congressional actions, news stories and other reports, but these provide only a dim picture of what actually went on. The world of the wiretapper is a dark one. He comes quietly, plies his trade in the shadows, and steals away. As a result, evidence of tapping can be accumulated only where the practice has been exposed.

In 1939, a Post Office inspector testified that he had been tapping regularly for twenty to twenty-five years. Three years later, Assistant Solicitor General Oscar Cox was telling a House committee that during World War I "there was much abuse of the wiretapping privilege or power, if you call it such, where subordinate officials on their own in many cases felt that it was necessary to tap wires beyond what, during a war, a conscientious prosecutor would think necessary in terms of the best interests of the people." These words contain the nexus of the problem.

During World War I, the government took control of our nation's telephone and telegraph systems. To protect the people, Congress made it a crime for any lines to be tapped "during the period of governmental operation." When the war ended, control reverted to private ownership, and the wiretap law became inoperative.

Soon after the Armistice, a public scare arose over the activities of political extremists, both anarchists and Communists. Bombs were sent through the mail to prominent persons and, even though most of these were intercepted, the news made frightening headlines. On the evening of June 2, 1919, a stranger started up the steps to the house of the new U.S. Attorney General, A. Mitchell Palmer, carrying a parcel. In it was a bomb that exploded prematurely. The explosion blew the windows out of nearby homes, one of which was occupied at the time by Assistant Secretary of the Navy Franklin D. Roosevelt.

Some time earlier, William B. Wilson, Secretary of Labor, then responsible for administering the immigration laws, had decided that Communist aliens were subject to deportation under these laws. With public emotion running high, Attorney General Palmer decided that one solution to the problem of "radicals" was to deport as many politically questionable aliens as possible.

More than five thousand arrest warrants were issued, based on information provided largely by undercover informants. On the evening of January 2, 1920, simultaneous mass raids were carried out in thirty-three cities. Arrested persons were herded together in vans and taken to local detention centers. Somewhere between eight and twelve thousand people were picked up. Some were known or suspected Communist aliens, and some were not.

At the centers, Bureau of Investigation agents interrogated those detained. Efforts were made to match the arrested persons to their warrants. Where there were no warrants, the authorizations for arrest were asked for and issued *post factum*. Those who were found to be citizens, and some aliens, were released within the first few days. However, great numbers were held for deportation. The conditions under which the victims were held is one of the stains on our record as a democratic nation.

The Assistant Secretary of Labor, Louis F. Post, on reviewing the records of those held for deportation, began to doubt such wholesale participation in a conspiracy to overthrow the government. After careful investigation, he canceled hundreds of the warrants. Many of the aliens, while members of the Communist Party, had no knowledge of its doctrine. Many more automatically became Communists when the Socialist Party split and the local Socialist groups to which they belonged became affiliated with the Communist Party. Many of the aliens were uneducated and spoke little English; to them, the Communist meeting hall was a convenient social club, a nice place to meet other newcomers to this country, to share common interests and memories.

Because of Post's courage in opposing the Attorney General, he was threatened with impeachment. But thanks to his review of the situation, only about five hundred persons were ultimately deported out of the thousands of men and women arrested in the raid.

In the course of this trampling on human rights, it is apparent that wiretapping was used by the Justice Department, nor was this all. During a House debate in 1954, Congressman Chet Holifield of California, referring to this era, spoke of the ". . . shameful public spectacle of the Department of Justice . . . infringing upon civil liberties of hundreds of citizens. . . . [Palmer] and his men would go into newspaper offices and tear up type, destroy the type, and throw the printing machinery out into the street. He did that against the liberal papers that they disagreed with. I could go on for a long time and tell you some of the crimes that they committed."

Under President Harding, Harry M. Daugherty succeeded Palmer as Attorney General, but he was no great improvement. The activities of the Bureau of Investigation now became largely political, centering upon labor organizations. In 1924, a Senate committee investigating Daugherty's curious inefficiency in connection with the Teapot Dome oil scandal, discovered that labor was not the only concern of the Justice Department's Bureau of Investigation. It had also spied on members of Congress. A former agent testified that he had searched the offices of Senator Robert M. La Follette to ascertain how much the Senator knew about the Teapot Dome bribe. The offices of other Senators and Congressmen had also been searched.

The testimony before this committee revealed a lack of

central control and discipline within the Bureau. Politics and patronage were overriding issues. While all this was coming to light, Daugherty left office. He was succeeded by Harlan F. Stone.

Attorney General Stone brought with him a new era of responsible government service and dedication to Constitutional principles. He reorganized the Bureau of Investigation. Its concerns were now strictly confined to violations of federal law: unqualified personnel were replaced by agents who had a legal education or a knowledge of accounting, and a system of rigid inspection and training was instituted. Playing politics was out. It was Harlan Stone who appointed J. Edgar Hoover as Director of the Investigation Bureau. The groundwork laid by Stone and the administration of Hoover have made the FBI the most generally respected law-enforcement agency in the United States.

The new Attorney General took one more significant step. He banned the use of wiretapping by the Bureau, but this ban lasted for only seven years.

Appearing before a House subcommittee on December 2, 1929, soon after William Mitchell became Attorney General, Director Hoover presented his views on wiretapping: "We have a very definite rule in the Bureau that any employee engaging in wiretapping will be dismissed. . . . While it may not be illegal, I think it is unethical, and it is not permitted under the regulations by the Attorney General."

The pertinent regulation was contained in the manual governing the operations of the Bureau. It read, "Unethical tactics: Wiretapping, entrapment, or the use of any other improper, illegal, or unethical tactics in procuring information in connection with investigative activity will not be tolerated by the Bureau."

The Justice Department ban on the use of wiretapping applied only to the Bureau. If other government departments or agencies had obtained wiretap evidence, there was no regulation against its use by the Justice Department in prosecuting a case. During the seven-year period in which this activity was banned in the Bureau, other federal law-enforcement agencies were busily at work with wiretaps.

Not long after World War I, Prohibition became the law of the land. The purpose of this law was highly moral, but by the way it was enforced, it seemed to be directed considerably lower. Here is Congressman Tarver—a supporter of Prohibition, incidentally—crying out against law-enforcement agents in 1933: "Those who believe in Prohibition will not help their cause by undertaking to back up rotten and inefficient enforcement . . . inefficient and corrupt agents must be gotten rid of, and methods of enforcement adopted . . . which will be decent and entitled to the backing of decent people."

Initially, the Prohibition Bureau was in the Treasury Department and was thus free to wiretap. For several years little public attention was paid to Prohibition wiretapping, but, in 1928, a Supreme Court case, *Olmstead* vs. *United States,* brought the matter into full public view. The case involved a major bootlegging operation that had been set up in Seattle. In their investigation, federal agents had tapped telephones and made notes of conversations overheard.

At the trial, the defense objected to admission of the

wiretap evidence on the grounds that it was obtained in violation of the Fourth Amendment,* and that its use in court would be contrary to the Fifth Amendment.† This was overruled by the trial court.

The Supreme Court sustained the judgment of the trial court, holding that wiretapping was not subject to the Fourth and Fifth Amendments. This decision set the stage for the legal confusion that has surrounded wiretapping and bugging in the ensuing years. The immediate effect of the case was to focus attention on the wiretap activities of the Prohibition Bureau, and to give rise to a Congressional effort to ban such activities. In 1931 and 1932, amendments were offered in the House to prohibit use of funds for wiretapping. They were defeated, but public support for such restraints continued to build.

In 1930, the Prohibition Bureau had been transferred from the Treasury Department to the Justice Department. At that time, Attorney General Mitchell had found himself faced with a contradictory situation within his Department: one bureau was using wiretaps while in another it was prohibited. He resolved the conflict by adopting the following regulation, applicable to both bureaus: "Wiretapping: Telephone or telegraph wires shall not be tapped unless prior authorization of the Director of the Bureau has been secured."

In 1932, the Prohibition Bureau revealed to a Senate subcommittee that all the Bureau's tapping was done by a special agency force of 188 men, concentrating its work in

* For text of the Fourth Amendment, see p. 26.

† The pertinent part of the Fifth Amendment reads: No person . . . shall be compelled in any criminal case to be a witness against himself. . . .

major cities. A detailed description of the procedure followed by the Bureau in approving wiretaps was offered by its Director, Col. Amos W. W. Woodcock, after which he added: "I am frank to say that this question of wiretapping has never registered any sense of disapproval in my mind at all." A wiretap ban, he said, "would grant an almost practical immunity to the large gangs and 'interests' in conspiracies." This argument remains traditional with government apologists for invasions of individual privacy.

Despite the strong protests of the Prohibition Bureau, Congress approved a ban on prohibition-case wiretapping in March, 1933. It was in the same year, incidentally, that Congressman Fred A. Britten expounded the views of many citizens when he referred to employees of the Bureau as "clerks, snoopers, mattress friskers, men who obtain evidence by tapping telephone wires and buying liquor."

In the summer of 1933, the Prohibition Bureau and the Bureau of Investigation were consolidated into the Division of Investigation, under Director Hoover. Then, in December, the Twenty-first Amendment ended Prohibition.

For a time, things seemed quiet on the federal wiretap front. By the mid-1930's however, the situation changed. Many federal agencies were trying their hand at wiretapping, and some of these activities were beginning to appear on the public record. Although our current federal law prohibiting wiretapping was passed by Congress in 1934, it was 1939 before the Supreme Court had defined its application to federal agents specifically enough to force their wiretap activities underground.

From 1937 to 1939, federal courts decided at least nine

cases involving Treasury Department wiretapping. By 1938, accounts of tapping by the FBI were on the record in federal court. A Senate hearing conducted by Senator La Follette in 1937, had revealed a disturbing association between federal law-enforcement agencies and the Pinkerton Detective Agency. Company officials assured the Senators that Pinkerton agents did not use wiretaps or similar practices *unless they were working with police, or state, or federal officials.* A Pinkerton vice-president volunteered that "I do not think it is uncommon to tap telephone wires by the police departments and the Federal authorities; for that matter, I think it is quite common."

The public record shows that, during the period from 1934 to 1939, a number of federal law-enforcement agencies—the Post Office and the Department of the Interior, too—engaged in the tapping of wires. Among the crimes against which the taps were used were mail fraud, prostitution, smuggling of alcoholic beverages and narcotics, and fraud by government employees. It seems safe to conclude that, during this period, wiretapping was a routine law-enforcement technique among federal agencies. The fiery debates in Congress over Prohibition wiretapping had been forgotten or were judged to be aimed at Prohibition enforcement only.

The present federal wiretap law prohibits, without the consent of the sender, the interception and divulgence of telephone communications. This wiretap provision, which is contained in Section 605 of the Federal Communications Act of 1934, became law without fanfare or debate. If any of the federal agencies tapping away at the time noticed the enactment of the ban, they probably assumed it did not apply to federal law-enforcement activities.

This situation was sharply changed in 1937 by the Supreme Court decision in the first Nardone case. The Court held that federal wiretapping was illegal too, and such evidence could not be used in federal court. Government law-enforcement officials immediately began to probe the loopholes in Section 605, seeking some means of continuing their wiretapping legally, as well as having the information so obtained accepted by the courts.

Two Supreme Court decisions in 1939 further narrowed the legitimate range of government snoopers. In the second Nardone case, it was held that evidence obtained through wiretap leads, like wiretap evidence itself, could not be used in federal courts. And in the Weiss case, Section 605 was construed to apply to intrastate calls as well as those across state lines. The Court also held that the consent required to tap legally must be given voluntarily and in advance. These decisions specifically closed the door on any possibility of legal wiretapping.

Shortly after these two decisions, Robert Jackson became Attorney General. On March 18, 1940, he announced his reinstatement of the wiretap ban which had existed prior to 1931. Further, the statement said that no case originating in or investigated by *any* department of the government would be presented to a grand jury or otherwise prosecuted if it had been developed in whole or part by wiretapping. The statement concluded:

> . . . it is believed by the Attorney General and the Director of the Bureau that the discredit and suspicion of the law-

enforcing branch which arises from the occasional use of wiretapping more than offsets the good which is likely to come to it [*sic*]. We have therefore completely abandoned the practice as to the Department of Justice.

In a limited class of cases, such as kidnapping, extortion, and racketeering . . . it is the opinion of the present Attorney General . . . that wiretapping should be authorized under some appropriate safeguard. . . . [This] cannot be done unless Congress sees fit to modify the existing statutes.

Publicly, this situation lasted about a year; actually, it lasted only six weeks.

On May 21, 1940, President Roosevelt sent the following confidential memorandum to Jackson:

I am convinced that the Supreme Court never intended any dictum in the particular case which it decided to apply to grave matters involving the defense of the Nation.

It is of course well known that certain other nations have been engaged in the organization of propaganda of so-called fifth columns in other countries and in preparation for sabotage, as well as in actual sabotage.

You are therefore authorized and directed in such cases as you may approve, after investigation of the need in each case, to authorize the necessary investigating agents that they are at liberty to secure information by listening devices directed to conversations or other communications of persons suspected of subversive activities against the Government of the United States, including suspected spies. You are requested furthermore to limit these investigations so conducted to a minimum and to limit them insofar as possible to aliens.

Wiretapping was resumed under the authority of the memorandum which today remains the basic authorization for FBI tapping in national security cases. The existence of the memorandum was not made public for nine years, despite subsequent acknowledgments by Robert Jackson and his successor, Francis Biddle, that the FBI was indeed wiretapping in national security and kidnaping cases.

The reasons for President Roosevelt's action in giving permission for wiretapping are clear. At the time, Hitler had defeated Western Europe and there was deep concern that England might soon be invaded. This would have left only the United States to stand against him. In the face of this very real danger, wiretapping was authorized.

Throughout the war years, Congress continued to wrestle with the issue. Bills were passed back and forth across the floor, with attempts being made to legalize wiretapping in cases involving espionage, sabotage, kidnaping, extortion, and violations of the narcotics laws. At the beginning, Congress did not know that wiretapping was already being used in espionage cases under the memorandum.

In a letter to Congressman Thomas Eliot in connection with one such bill, President Roosevelt made the point that wiretapping should be made lawful in cases involving those "who today are engaged in espionage or sabotage against the United States. . . . There is only one domestic crime which ought possibly to be included: that is kidnapping."

This letter was sent in 1941 and, shortly afterwards, Attorney General Jackson sent a letter of his own to the House Judiciary Committee, setting forth for the first time the Justice Department doctrine which has cut the heart out of Section 605. The letter said:

> There is no Federal statute that prohibits or punishes wire tapping alone. The only offense under the present law is to intercept any communication *and divulge or publish the same* [italics added]. Any person, with no risk of penalty, may tap telephone wires and eavesdrop on his competitor, employee, workman, or others, and act upon what he hears or make [any] use of it that does not involve divulging or publication. . . . The courts do not stop people from tapping wires—no one has ever been, or under present law, could be, convicted of that by itself. What has been stopped is the use of the evidence to enforce the laws against criminals. . . . These decisions lay down rules of evidence. But since our use of this method would have as its chief purpose the proof of a case against criminals, the practical effect of these decisions is to make wire tapping unavailing to law-enforcement officers, although still useful to those who make private use of it. For this reason it was discontinued by the Department of Justice.

Jackson noted in the same letter that he had recently ordered a wiretap in a kidnaping case.

Giving testimony before this same Committee was James L. Fly, Chairman of the Federal Communications Commission, who strongly disagreed with the Jackson contention that wiretapping itself was legal. He vigorously opposed legislation that might permit it, and recommended instead that the prohibition in Section 605 should be tightened. He also argued that wiretap legislation would hinder rather than promote national defense. The pending bill to legalize tapping was rejected by the House.

On December 7, 1941, the Japanese struck Pearl Harbor, and the United States entered World War II. Despite the sense of national emergency, another measure to authorize wiretapping introduced shortly after our entry into the war met the fate of earlier bills. The Supreme Court, on April 27, 1942, handed down two more wiretap decisions. Although neither case affected matters of national defense, the Court for the first time limited the scope of Section 605's protection of telephone privacy.

In the first case, *Goldman* vs. *United States,* federal agents had made use of a detectaphone, a device for listening through walls. It had permitted them to overhear conversations taking place in the defendant's office, including some over the telephone. The Court held that Section 605 did not prohibit listening in on one end of a phone conversation, and that the use of the detectaphone did not violate the Fourth Amendment.

The second, the Goldstein case, involved the fact that certain government witnesses in a mail fraud case had been confronted with recordings of their telephone calls before they decided to turn state's evidence. The defendant who had not been a party to any of the intercepted calls objected to their testimony. The Supreme Court held that only persons who are a party to intercepted telephone conversations have a right to object, under Section 605, to the use of wiretaps.

This second decision was of special comfort to the Justice Department, since it seemed to bolster the position that wiretapping in itself was legal.

Two months after Harry S. Truman became President in 1945, Tom C. Clark took over as Attorney General. In a letter to President Truman on July 17, 1946, he set out the Roosevelt confidential memorandum in full. And then he wrote: "This directive . . . is being followed currently in this department. . . . It seems to me imperative to use [wiretapping] . . . in cases vitally affecting the domestic security, or where human life is in jeopardy." President Truman wrote at the foot of the letter, "I concur."

In 1948, John L. Lewis, President of the United Mine Workers, charged Clark with sending FBI agents to tap UMW telephones. "Surely ol' Tom hasn't forgotten the day he sent one of his gumshoe men in to tap our telephones in our office and our boys threw him out on his ear," Lewis said, adding, "They caught him right at the control box in the basement, tapping, and they threw him out." Clark reportedly answered that no tap was necessary because Lewis roared so loud.

A series of articles on wiretapping appeared in the *New York Star* that same year. It was alleged that FBI taps had been placed on the telephones of such well-known persons as Colonel Robert McCormick, James A. Farley, Jesse Jones, Cissie Patterson, Harry Bridges, Philip Murray, and, once again, Lewis. The articles also charged that the FBI had tapped the phones of hundreds of other Americans, including Senators, Congressmen, admirals, and union leaders. The *New York Times* inquired but was unable to learn from the FBI whether they had tapped or not.

About this time, there was much controversy over the Federal Employee Loyalty Program. On March 22, 1947, President Truman issued an executive order, known as the Loyalty Order, and this became a focal point for public discussion. In an article published in 1948 in the *Yale Law Journal,* Thomas Emerson and David Helfeld examined the loyalty program in depth. Director Hoover considered many of the article's references to the FBI "obviously incomplete and distorted," and he wrote to the *Journal* to that effect, making a number of specific observations and comments.

The article had said, "Although the FBI denies that it taps telephones, instances of that practice have been reported." Hoover replied: "I challenge the authors to come forward with one single instance wherein a telephone was tapped in the investigation of a Federal Employee Loyalty Program case. It is no secret that the FBI does tap telephones in a very limited type of cases with the express approval in each instance of the Attorney General . . . but only in cases involving espionage, sabotage, grave risks to internal security, or when human lives are in jeopardy. This is never done in the investigation of the loyalty of Federal employees. This unsubstantiated statement by the authors typifies their obvious efforts to discredit the work of the FBI in Loyalty cases."

In their own reply, also in the *Journal,* the authors stood by their original remarks, and claimed that the Hoover statement on wiretapping was self-contradictory. Hoover returned to the fray once more, this time making a reference to President Roosevelt's confidential memorandum of 1940, apparently the first public comment about the memorandum. This exchange included another revelation: it was the first public acknowledgment of FBI wiretapping by a Justice Department official since 1942.

March 4, 1949, witnessed the beginning of what was to become the biggest free-for-all in the history of federal wiretapping. On that day, the FBI arrested Judith Coplon, an employee of the Justice Department, and Valentine A. Gubitchev, a Russian national employed by the United Nations. They were both charged with espionage.

The story began in the summer of 1943, when Miss Coplon went to work for the Justice Department in New York. In 1945, she was transferred to Washington where, in time, she worked in the Internal Security Section, examining FBI reports on Russian agents and Communists.

A "confidential informant" sparked an FBI investigation of Miss Coplon. In January, 1949, a wiretap was installed on her home telephone in Washington, and a week later she was followed by agents when she made a brief trip to New York. She was observed there in the company of Mr. Gubitchev. In the same month, taps were installed on her office telephone at the Justice Department, on her family's telephone in New York, and on Gubitchev's home telephone. In another New York visit, she was seen to pass some object or material to Gubitchev. On March 3, she informed her supervisor at the Department that she was making another trip to New York the next day. The next morning he gave her three memoranda which were actually decoys.

In New York later that day, she was trapped by FBI agents in the act of passing papers to Gubitchev, and they were both arrested. The papers being transmitted included information abstracted from the three decoys that had been handed to her "officially" that morning.

Miss Coplon was indicted by Federal Grand Juries for violations of the espionage laws in both Washington and New York. Her Washington trial began in April and lasted for more than two months. The taps on her Washington telephones (home and office) had been removed, but the one on her family's telephone in New York was continued until some two weeks after the Washington trial began.

During the trial, the defense inquired as to whether the government had used wiretapping. The Court, however, sustained the prosecution's view that this was merely a reconnaissance technique and the taps were not revealed. On June 30, Judith Coplon was convicted.

Her New York trial was not scheduled for some time yet, and so the FBI reinstalled the tap on her New York family residence on July 12. During the autumn, the defense filed with the New York federal court a pretrial motion on the use of wiretapping. A hearing was held, and the whole story of the wiretaps was brought out. It was learned that fifty FBI agents had joined in keeping twenty-four-hour-a-day coverage on the four taps. The trial judge was highly critical, expressing his reactions in these words: "The fact that these interceptions were carried on under written authorization of the Attorney General imparts no sanctity to them: they remain unlawful and prohibited."

The Court did not grant the defense motion to dismiss the indictment, however, but it did rule all wiretap evidence inadmissible. It also disallowed all evidence obtained as a result of the taps, except where there was an independent source for such evidence.

The New York trial of Judith Coplon and Valentine Gubitchev began shortly after this hearing. The Court ordered the government to turn over to the defense all discs and all written records of the taps, so that it could determine if any evidence came solely or primarily from them. It allowed the deletion of certain passages which both it and the government felt would endanger national security if disclosed. The Court examined the deletions and found they contained no leads to evidence. The defense was not permitted to examine the deletions. Miss Coplon was again convicted of espionage.

She appealed, and the FBI's use of wiretapping was fatal to both convictions. The District of Columbia Court of Appeals returned its case to the trial court to determine whether the taps had monitored conversations between Miss Coplon and her attorney, either before the trial or during it. The Second Circuit Court of Appeals reversed the New York conviction because her arrest was illegal, and because the trial court relied on evidence it had seen and heard but the defense had not.

But before these appeals were heard, the story took a strange turn. On February 10, 1950, the Soviet Union charged that the FBI was tapping United Nations telephone lines. After much tugging and hauling through the press, the Russian charges came to nothing. On March 3, Trygve Lie, Secretary General of the United Nations, sent to the Soviet Union a complete and formal denial. There was no doubt that the public evidence of FBI wiretapping in the Coplon case, in which Gubitchev, of course, figured, was the basic cause for this diversion.

In 1957, years after the event, another Attorney General, Herbert Brownell, announced that Judith Coplon would not be tried for espionage again. Whatever information the government had been able to obtain through wiretapping was dearly come by: it had cost the government its case.

The disclosures in the Coplon case brought renewed

questions concerning wiretap activities by the FBI and other federal investigative agencies. A representative of the Treasury Department stated that his department did not use such methods, and the Postmaster General refused to comment on the subject.

Following the reversal of the New York Coplon conviction, Attorney General McGrath sent to Congress a proposed wiretap bill, pointing out that new legislation was sorely needed. He referred to cases in past years that could not be prosecuted under existing law, and the Coplon case was, of course, one such example. No action was taken on this bill.

The year 1953 brought a new Administration, a new Congress, and a new effort to obtain wiretap legislation. McCarthyism was riding high, and public sentiment was warm toward any measure that could be given an anti-Communist label. The new Attorney General, Herbert Brownell, sent to the Congress a bill "to authorize the use in criminal proceedings in Federal Courts of information obtained by intercepting of communications in the course of investigations relating to the protection of the national security or defense." To insure widespread emotional support for the bill, it was dubbed the "Anti-Traitor" bill. It passed the House, but no action was taken in the Senate.

Two issues seem to have been responsible for the bill's failure to pass. First, it contained no provisions to clarify the law as it applied to private wiretapping. Second, and probably more important, was the question of requiring court orders to tap. Such a requirement, which many members of Congress considered an indispensable qualification in any bill that would permit wiretapping, was not included. At one point, Congressman Kenneth Keating, one of the leaders in the push for the legislation, told the House that Director Hoover and the Attorney General had told him they preferred no bill at all to a bill that required court orders.

While national attention was focused on internal security matters, federal wiretappers continued to make lavish use of their talents. As could be expected, the tapping was not limited to national security. An exchange between Senator Paul Douglas and Senator Wayne Morse on the Senate floor in June, 1954, provided one glimpse of what things were like during this period. Senator Morse was speaking on wiretapping, and Senator Douglas asked him if attorneys who were defending persons accused in federal courts in tax and other matters had ever suggested that their wires were being tapped. Senator Morse replied: "Only last week a constituent . . . was in my office. He was . . . concerned about a tax matter in which he is satisfied that he is the victim of such methods." Then Senator Douglas said, "I have talked with a number of reputable attorneys in this country representing clients in tax matters and in certain criminal cases. They have said that they are almost certain that their wires have been tapped continuously and that therefore the defense which they intended to put up in court was known to the prosecution."

In 1954, the technique of listening in on telephone calls with the knowledge of one party to the call seems to have become a routine law-enforcement practice. From 1954 to 1957, at least a dozen cases were decided by federal courts in which this technique had been used. In nine of the cases, the practice was upheld by the courts. Most of these cases were narcotics violations; others included perjury and racketeering.

With the official censure of Senator Joseph McCarthy in December, 1954, the nation began to shift to a more even keel. One proof was the fact that the number of FBI wiretaps declined substantially. In 1950, there were almost 170 internal security wiretaps in operation at any one time. By 1958, there were only about half as many.

In November, 1957, the Appalachin meeting of the leaders of organized crime brought about a new crusading spirit for the legalization of wiretapping. It also brought an increase in the illegal use of wiretaps and electronic snooping. Around this time, William Rogers became Attorney General and, in response to Appalachin, he set up a Special Group on Organized Crime. But he requested no special wiretap legislation from Congress, preferring to rest on the pragmatic tradition he had inherited from his predecessors. He submitted other bills to Congress, however, that would facilitate a war on crime, but these bills were not passed.

The story was different when the next Attorney General arrived on the scene. Robert Kennedy requested a similar package of bills—they were enacted—and also instituted the Organized Crime Drive (see Chapter 3). This was designed to bring all federal law enforcement agencies together in a coordinated battle against organized crime. He also asked for a wiretap bill early in 1962, but this request met the same fate as those that had preceded it.

Newspaper stories and official reports have revealed that, in today's world, snooping whether by wiretap or electronics has become commonplace.

In 1964, Secretary of Labor Willard Wirtz announced that he had banned the use of telephone recording and other eavesdropping devices in his department. This bright spot, however, was a lonely beacon in a generally bleak landscape. Because of the evident seriousness of the situation, the Senate Subcommittee on Administrative Practice and Procedure in that year began its investigation of government practices that invade privacy. The investigation has not only substantiated the most pessimistic views but has revealed a degree of snooping that defies even the most cynical imagination.

The war between what is right and what is "necessary" continues. In 1928, Supreme Court Justice Brandeis offered these words of advice: "Experience should teach us to be most on our guard to protect liberty when the Government's purposes are beneficient. Men born to freedom are naturally alert to repel invasion of their liberty by evil-minded rulers. The greatest dangers to liberty lurk in insidious encroachments by men of zeal, well-meaning but without understanding."

6

The Government's "Private" Eye

ON THE AFTERNOON of February 5, 1964, Mrs. Marie Bolan was handed her mail by the substitute carrier on the route. At the same time, he handed her a document, saying that he didn't know what it was but perhaps she should have that, too. It was a Post Office form dated March, 1963, directing the mail carrier to submit to his supervisor all first class mail addressed to Thomas and Marie Bolan. It was marked "Confidential—Do not reveal this to addressee or other unauthorized persons," and was endorsed "Indefinite until canceled."

Only by this fluke did the Bolans learn that their mail had been watched for almost a year by the federal government. This technique is known as a mail cover. By means of it, the Post Office systematically records all visible information on all mail going to a particular addressee. It then turns the information over to the government agency—federal, state, or local—that requested the cover.

Thomas Bolan, an attorney, was then representing his law partner, Roy Cohn, who had been indicted by a federal grand jury for perjury and obstruction of justice. Bolan immediately requested a federal court hearing on the government's use of mail covers. He alleged they had been placed not only on his home mail but on that of Roy Cohn and of their joint law office as well.

At this hearing, the judge refused the defense motion to dismiss the case, but he said: "I think it is a shocking thing for the U.S. Attorney's office to put a mail watch on the mail of an attorney for a defendant after he has been indicted. . . . I think that smacks of Russia rather than the United States."

The Cohn case was one of the first to be discussed in detail when the Senate Subcommittee on Administrative Practice and Procedure opened its public hearings in February, 1965, on government invasions of individual privacy. Although Congress has struggled for many years with the policy and constitutional issues raised by wiretapping, it had never before made any comprehensive effort to explore official use of this and many other privacy-assaulting techniques. Despite the furtive nature of the practices, and a general lack of cooperation on the part of government agencies, the Subcommittee was able to document a wide range of such activities.

The overzealous government agent is very much with us. He often receives not only encouragement but even leadership from his superiors as he creeps in and out of other people's private lives. The Subcommittee obtained proof of many instances in which federal agents had violated the Constitution, federal law, state law, and even their own agency regulations. Sometimes they had violated all four at the same time. The average citizen has been subject to government snooping in his home, at work, and at church. Even in his direct contacts with the government, he has been the victim of the hidden eye and ear. His mail, telephone calls, and conversations with his wife, his doctor, his lawyer, and his minister, are considered fair game by government snoopers. Here is a brief overview of what the Subcommittee's findings reveal, and the steps that have been taken in some cases to correct such abuses:

Tampering With the Mails—"Official": A Postal Regulation of 1893 authorized postmasters to furnish officers of the law any exterior information obtainable from envelopes, to aid in discovering a fugitive from justice. This practice, however, went almost unnoticed until 1954, when it was discovered that mail cover orders had been placed on a U.S. Senator and members of his staff. Ironically, the senator was Joseph McCarthy, for whom Roy Cohn was then working.

A special committee, looking into the matter, found the covers had been placed on the basis of a letter to the Post Office that bore a facsimile stamp signature of the chairman of a Senate subcommittee that was investigating certain of Senator McCarthy's activities. Neither the chairman nor any of his colleagues knew of the letter or the covers. It was the work of an overzealous subcommittee staff member. Regulations governing mail covers were so lax that a facsimile stamp signature alone was sufficient authorization to arrange for placing them on a Senator and his staff. When the story came to light in 1954, the Post Office tightened its regulations somewhat.

The subsequent revelations in the Cohn case, coupled with the introduction of legislation to ban all mail covers, stimulated further tightening of requirements. But at public hearings conducted by the Senate Subcommittee on Administrative Practice and Procedure, postal officials admitted to conducting about one thousand mail covers a month.

The Post Office witnesses conceded there was no statute specifically authorizing the use of mail covers. Instead, postal employees had relied on custom and usage for over seventy years and the authority of the Postmaster General to run this service. They cited two Court of Appeals decisions which they claimed upheld the legality of the practice. Actually, however, neither of these cases addressed itself to the basic question of the Department's authority to conduct covers. The law is far from definite on this point.

Because mail covers, like wiretaps, are not discovered except by accident, the Senate Subcommittee asked the Postmaster General to produce the names of the 24,000 victims of such covers during the two preceding years. The Postmaster General refused to comply with the request. It would, he thought, violate the civil liberties of that large number of people in the group who were completely innocent of any crime. For some mysterious reason, he appeared unaware of the damage to civil liberties in the first place by placing the covers on persons presumed innocent to begin with. Out of this conflict came a compromise. The Subcommittee agreed to withdraw its request for the list, and new postal regulations placed significant limitations on the use of mail covers.

Throughout these hearings, the Post Office witnesses time and again told the Subcommittee that the seal on first class mail was sacred. They vowed it was never opened except with a search warrant or at the dead letter office in accordance with the law. Despite the stream of solemn avowals, it was soon learned that first class mail has been opened.

Representative Durwood Hall of Missouri gave the Subcommittee a lead to a practice known as a "mail levy." The IRS is authorized by statute to seize property belonging to a delinquent taxpayer. Certain items are exempt from seizure, but mail was not specifically one of them. This lack of specific reference to first class mail led the IRS to evolve the rewarding theory that mail was fair game. Between 1962 and 1964, there were thirty-four cases in which the Post Office had turned over personal first class mail to the IRS for opening.

What does the Constitution say about this? The U.S. Supreme Court, in 1877, decided as follows: "No law of Congress can place in the hands of officials connected with the Postal Service any authority to invade the secrecy of letters in . . . sealed packages in the mail. And all regulations as to mail matter of this kind must be in subordination to the great principle embodied in the Fourth Amendment to the Constitution."

It is hard to imagine how the Court could have been more explicit. But the IRS did not seem to get the point. In putting through its mail levies, it continued to flout the decision of the Court—and the Post Office acquiesced. To close the door on the practice once and for all, Congress passed a bill in 1965 specifically exempting mail from the levy power of the IRS.

During the Senate Subcommittee hearings, the story was

told of a Russian-language bookstore in California which counted among its customers the U.S. Army Language School, as well as a number of universities. The books and materials the store ordered from the Soviet Union were seized by the Post Office when they came into this country. At one point, while the Army Language School was screaming for Russian-English dictionaries, each shipment ordered by the store was being systematically seized and destroyed by the postal authorities. Not only were the essential dictionaries seized but also books on the rodents of the U.S.S.R., and instructions on how to play the harmonica. This was part of a program of the Post Office and the Customs Bureau to control Communist propaganda entering the country.

For many years this propaganda-control program was carried out by the Post Office, as was the authorization of mail covers and mail levies, without any authority from the Congress. The program had been initiated in 1940 to stop the flow of Nazi propaganda into the United States. The Korean War and McCarthyism set up simultaneous pressures to strengthen this program with respect to Communist propaganda. Screening centers were set up at every port of entry, and the criteria became so loosely defined that the seizures noted above were encouraged to take place.

Because of the lunacy inherent in this situation, there were many complaints. The Post Office then revised its policy in such a way that addressees would be notified that the Post Office was holding mail considered to be Communist propaganda. This would be released on request by return post card. A person subscribing to a daily paper would, under a 1965 version of this policy, have to request each day's issue (seized, of course) from the Post Office with its separate daily post card. The program, discontinued by President Kennedy in 1961, had been reinstituted by Congress in 1962. During the summer of 1965, the Supreme Court held the entire program unconstitutional.

The Post Office and the Bureau of Customs continue, however, to scrutinize all mail arriving from foreign countries. The current ostensible purpose of this screening is to stop the flow of obscenity. The program against political propaganda was limited to open mail, but the obscenity program includes sealed mail as well. When a sealed letter or package is suspected of containing obscene material, request is made to the addressee for permission to open and inspect it. Without such permission, the mail is returned to the postal authorities of the originating country.

In another procedure, when the Post Office finds an outgoing letter addressed to a known foreign distributor of obscenity, it may stamp the letter "Unlawful" and return it to the sender.

But the Post Office Department's surveillance activities have not been limited to mail. Inspectors spend considerable time watching through peepholes as postal employees do their work. About a century ago, the Department began to install these peepholes, or "lookout galleries," in larger post offices to protect the mail from thefts by employees. Today, there are peepholes in over five thousand post offices, and they are being installed in all new offices that contain more than twenty employees.

Over the years, peepholes have been maintained in the men's rest rooms, and the men's and women's locker rooms, as well as the work rooms. Postal department witnesses argued before the Senate Subcommittee that this kind of surveillance was necessary if the more than one trillion dollars worth of items passing through the mails annually was to be adequately protected.

Patrick Nilan, of the United Federation of Postal Clerks, took the position that these peepholes "constitute a continuing invasion of privacy." It was also pointed out that the government paid almost $2.5 million a year to build and operate this "spying system, or about ten times the amount recovered from postal depredations."

Since the Senate Subcommittee investigation began, peepholes in men's rest rooms and women's locker rooms have been sealed, but they continue in use in work rooms, men's locker rooms, and men's and women's "swing" rooms (where postal employees gather between shifts).

After its review of Post Office abuses, the Senate Subcommittee moved on to other agencies and other privacy-invading practices. It was soon hip-high in a swamp of abusive police techniques, with little or no cooperation provided it by the offending agencies. There were a few lonely exceptions, such as the Coast Guard which quickly responded to suggestions as to how privacy in its facilities could be insured against invasion. The Food and Drug Administration, for one, was less than cooperative.

Eat What We Tell You: The FDA, perhaps confusing itself with some kind of national Mother, has sometimes gone overboard in telling Americans what they should and should not eat. If you use vitamins or dietary supplements, the FDA may refer to you as a "food faddist." In trying to drive such products off the market, it has subjected some individuals to trial by publicity, and has seized a number of books. Both these techniques appear to be standard weapons in the FDA arsenal.

One characteristic of the FDA stood out clearly in the Senate Subcommittee's investigation of its activities. Unlike other agencies, which were willing at least to reexamine abusive practices, this organization seemed to feel that it could do no wrong.

When the Food and Drug Act was passed in 1906, the agency had little difficulty proving that the claims of various elixirs as "cures" for a wide range of diseases were false. The medicine men, learning from their defeats, took their claims off the label and began to transfer them to promotional literature that was distributed separately. In 1938, Congress blocked this tactic by defining such literature as "labels," too. This persuaded the entrepreneurs to turn to oral promotion of their products. But today's medicine man is careful of what he says and how he says it. He does his lecturing in large auditoriums, at fairs and carnivals, and door-to-door. Before the magic of electronics was everywhere available, the FDA might have a stenographer in the promoter's or pitchman's audience, busily transcribing his wilder claims. But the FDA now uses the far more foolproof electronic snooping gear.

In addition to miniature transmitters and recorders, the FDA makes use of two-way radios and walkie-talkies, as well as devices for wiretapping. A. E. Rayfield, director of the agency's Bureau of Compliance, told the Senate Subcommittee that it sometimes records telephone calls between suspects and its undercover agents. But he denied that it ever taps telephone conversations to which it is not a party.

The testimony of FDA witnesses maintained that snooping gear is used only against drug peddlers, hoodlums, frauds, con men, and others who prey on the old, the innocent, and the ignorant. Instances have come to light, however, in which the FDA has been caught snooping into the private lives of more responsible citizens. One can hardly imagine two people less dangerous to the public safety than the two Kansas City schoolteachers mentioned in Chapter 1.

It should surprise no one that the prepared FDA testimony did not include another instance where inspectors were caught with a hidden tape recorder at work. This took place in 1962 in Yonkers, New York. Two FDA inspectors went to the plant of American Dietaids, Inc., to conduct a factory inspection. Federal law permits them to do this, but they are not authorized, in the course of such inspections, to see books and records or to ask questions. This may be done under the law only by a somewhat different procedure.

In the course of this inspection, however, the company's general manager discovered that one of the inspectors was carrying a concealed recorder in his brief case, and had been monitoring the entire inspection tour. He demanded that the tapes be turned over to him but the inspector refused. The use of hidden recorders, he explained, was now standard practice during factory inspections. Following this incident and the result of pressure from Congressmen, the Secretary of Health, Education, and Welfare issued a directive, in 1962, banning the use of concealed recording devices during factory inspections.

This situation spotlights the difficulty involved in controlling the uses of electronic snooping. The government agency claims to be using snooping gear only "in extreme circumstances," and only against the enemies of society. Yet example after example is discovered, usually by accident, in which such equipment and methods have been used against average citizens.

As an aftermath of the Senate Subcommittee's investigation, the FDA saw no need to consider whether it should change some of its practices. Instead, some nameless FDA official released a statement to the press in which it was claimed that "The committee (i.e., the Senate Subcommittee on Administrative Practice and Procedure) let well-known quacks and crackpots fill the record with their charges."

Who were these witnesses labeled "quacks and crackpots"? One was Ellis Arnall, former Governor of Georgia who has served the federal government as Director of the Office of Price Administration and worked for the U.N. as a member of the Committee on UNESCO. Another was Oscar Brinkman, an attorney who has three times served as counsel to Senate committees. He has also served as an attorney for the National Labor Relations Board and the Interstate Commerce Commission. A third was Carlton Fredericks, a recognized health lecturer and nutritionist who holds a Ph.D. in Public Health Education from New York University. In the eyes of the agency, all had committed the same crime—they had disagreed with the FDA.

No one denies the necessity to protect the general public from fraud in the area of health, but is that needed protection to be achieved mainly through the irresponsible use of invasion-of-privacy techniques and devices?

The Hunt For Money: The IRS is the largest federal law-enforcement agency, employing about 60,000 persons. Despite the thirty-year-old Treasury Department ban on wiretapping, the IRS has, as we know, been unable to rid itself of the habit of snooping. Through one witness, Owen Burke Yung, the Senate Subcommittee was able to trace continuous wiretapping and electronic snooping by the IRS from the early 1940's to the present. As Senior Coordinator of the IRS Intelligence Division in the national office, Yung is something of a Grand Old Man, a patriarch of pokers into other people's affairs. At the time he joined the IRS underground army, in 1942, he was assigned to the New York office. Working there, also, was William Mellin, so-called Dean of Wiretappers, whose sole duty at that time was to install taps and bugs for the IRS and other federal agencies.

In 1954, Mellin wrote a letter to a Senate committee that was holding hearings on a wiretap bill. Written primarily to support the view that law-enforcement wiretapping should be permitted only with court order, the letter contained some fascinating information on the life and times of a government snoop. Mellin wrote, "After five years of varied experience with the telephone company, including wiretapping, I devoted the rest of my life to the science of wiretapping for local, State, and Federal authorities . . . in the course of my long career, I have tapped in excess of 60,000 pairs of wires. . . .

". . . I have been on wiretaps for many years and on one particular case for more than five years.

"I can state the conclusion with the authority of my forty years experience as a wiretapper that I do not know of a single instance where any investigation in which I was engaged would have been hampered by the requirement of a court order if the court order were obtained within 48 hours from the time the decision was made to tap the wire."

These are the words of an expert, and they should be recalled by anyone who addresses himself to the issue of legalizing wiretapping and bugging.

Yung's experience with the IRS as a licensed Peeping Tom may not have reached the round numbers achieved by Mellin, but he was kept busy enough. Here are a few examples chosen at random from his extremely active and far-ranging career:

1957: A microphone and a tap were installed in the IRS office in Buffalo. This was done without the knowledge of any local IRS officials, including the District Director.

1958: Yung used a lock pick to break into the apartment of an IRS employee, after which he installed a microphone under a bookcase in the living room.

1964: At the request of the Pittsburgh office, Yung took equipment there for the purpose of installing transmitter wiretaps. He instructed local agents in the use of the equipment, and the taps were then installed by the local agents.

After listening to an impressive catalog of such activities, the Subcommittee chairman thought it reasonable to ask Yung how he justified his snooping activities in view of the fact that he had violated the U.S. Constitution, federal law, state law, and the regulations of his own Department of the Treasury. Yung told the Subcommittee that in

1955 he had been informed of a letter by the Deputy Commissioner of the IRS authorizing the Inspection Service to tap government telephones. An IRS attorney expressed the view at the same hearing that it was not clear what kind of tapping was actually banned by the 1938 regulation. As to Section 605, Yung seemed to rely on the Justice Department's interpretation that *divulgence* is necessary to establish a violation.

Yung also stated that he did not concern himself with state laws, because an Assistant Attorney General had advised him once that a "Federal officer in fulfulling his duties, even though he violates state law, it does not apply to Federal officers [*sic*]." The Senate Subcommittee took the opportunity to point out the danger of following this advice in its broadest sense.

Yung's attitude was summed up in a single statement: "I do not think any law-enforcement officer, sir, does this [wiretapping and bugging] with the intent to violate any criminal laws or any constitutional rights of anyone. I think they do it in their eagerness to obtain information about what is going on in the country and to try to make a better country."

It is highly informative to look at ways in which this "eagerness" expresses itself. Since 1956, Yung had served as an instructor at a government educational institution. This is the Treasury Department's Technical Investigative Aids School, a select study group conducted for two weeks each year in Washington. Here, agents from all branches of the Department are instructed in the use of "investigative aids."

This country is supposed to have one of the greatest educational systems in the world, but even those most appreciative of this will be disturbed to learn of some of the subjects taught at the Treasury Department school. They include wiretapping, bugging, lock-picking, the use of amplifier and recorder, ultraviolet light, and, of course, photography. The school's enrollment has usually run to about 30 agents annually and, by 1965, the IRS had over 120 agents who had completed their studies there. The diploma handed to each graduate of the school is probably unique in the world of pedagogy: a set of lock-picking tools to be carried back to the job.

It should be remembered that other agents attending this school for snoopers are from the Secret Service, Customs Bureau, Alcohol and Tobacco Tax Unit, Inspection Service, and the Narcotics Bureau.

It is the official line of the Treasury Department that wiretapping and bugging are taught for defensive purposes only. But several IRS witnesses, including Yung, admitted that the line between defensive and offensive use is thin, and that it has been crossed. The Department has not been able to offer any convincing explanation for the use of lock-picks and instruction in their use.

Some of the instructions contained in the IRS manual for agents should be of interest to the taxpayer. Agents are cautioned not to slink from place to place, but to "act natural." On the other hand, it also suggests the possible use of a woman's hat and scarf as disguises. One thoughtful hint recommended that "the possibility of examining the subject's luggage in the railroad station or on the train should not be overlooked." Another suggestion from the manual: "If the hotel management is cooperative, it may be possible to procure a room near the subject's which can be used as a base for technical surveillance." This last term was interpreted to mean "electronic surveillance." Another helpful hint: "The possibility of trash coverage and entries should not be overlooked." This provision, when taken in conjunction with the following one, seems to explain some of the gross invasions of privacy uncovered by the Subcommittee. "Use of equipment in surveillance may be of great help under the appropriate conditions as additional devices and aids. Microphone installations will often produce information of great value."

In at least one IRS district office, these suggestions have been made into a check list and agents are required, during an investigation, to check off each technique used.

Joseph Harmon, Deputy Chief of Intelligence for the IRS, admitted to the Subcommittee that he had known and approved of Owen Yung's wiretap activities since 1961. He said he had never discussed these activities with his superiors in the national office because "they would have said, 'You know the regulations, anybody who does this is on their own.'" He had discussed wiretapping with his superiors only on occasions when IRS agents had been caught, but he had never been reprimanded by them for his agents' activities.

The Constitution, federal and state law, and Department regulations place restrictions on the activities of IRS agents. Yet there is every indication that they were expected and even encouraged to wiretap, bug, or take other privacy-invading action if it was deemed necessary to prove a criminal case. Snooping devices were dispatched to the various districts by the national office, which was ready to provide expert assistance with its special equipment. All this was going on with the knowledge of highly placed IRS officials.

Clouding the picture even more for the agent was the emphasis on the Organized Crime Drive. Because of this program, traditional lines of command had been altered, and OCD efforts had been separated from other IRS operations. The differing line of authority tended to remove any objective control over OCD activities.

The Senate Subcommittee's 1965 hearings revealed numerous incidents in which it appears that the OCD label was used indiscriminately to allow agents to apply "no holds barred" investigative techniques. The "get your man at any cost" attitude emanating from the IRS national office in matters which could be covered by the Organized Crime Drive seems to have spread fairly wide at the local level. There was the prevalence of a disquieting attitude best expressed in the phrase, "I'm hitting him, so he must be guilty." Given this background of confusion in the chain of command, it is hardly surprising that the Subcommittee found many instances of invasion of privacy by IRS agents.

In Pittsburgh, the Subcommittee learned of a spying technique that has been practiced throughout the nation. One witness, a certified public accountant, told of discovering a two-way mirror in an IRS conference room. He was meeting in the room with a taxpayer, his attorney, and two IRS agents. Someone accidentally bumped a picture of the Statue of Liberty hanging on the wall; it fell, exposing the two-way mirror behind it. Also, in the conference room, although not discovered at the time, was a concealed microphone hidden in a wallplug.

Less than a month after this testimony, Commissioner Sheldon Cohen provided the Senate Subcommittee with a list of ten cities in which there was an IRS conference room with a two-way mirror, and twenty-two cities in which there was a conference room with a concealed bug. These bugs had been hidden above windows, inside dummy thermostats and dummy telephones, as well as in wall plugs.

Internal Revenue Service witnesses explained that these odd examples of democracy in action had been used to record interviews with informers, with persons who might be expected to offer a bribe, with known criminals, and with any IRS employees in internal security cases who might become "emotional." There was no evidence to substantiate that the equipment was used to eavesdrop on supposedly private conversations between taxpayers and their attorneys or accountants when they were alone together in these rooms, but the potential for such abuse was certainly present.

On learning of these installations, Commissioner Cohen ordered that all permanent installations of this nature be removed. He did not ban the use of temporary installations in limited circumstances, however.

On the basis of cases heard by the Subcommittee, it is possible to consider the IRS the agency that engaged in a maximum of privacy invasion to achieve a minimum of worthwhile results.

In one case involving the possibility of tax evasion, the IRS joined hands with the Pennsylvania police in the use of a pen register and taps on the telephones suspected of being used for call-girl activities. On an evening in October, 1963, IRS agents accompanied state police to the home of the suspected head of this prostitution operation. Armed with a search warrant, the men fine-combed the premises and seized everything that might prove useful in convicting the owner of tax evasion. They also arrested two women who were in the house. At the time of the raid, other state police were visiting bars and rounding up suspected prostitutes. The suspected head of the operation was eventually charged with evasion of taxes, but here again we have the old story: because of the taint of wiretapping, much of the evidence was suppressed and nothing came of the case.

The accounts of so many men sneaking, creeping, and peeping around the margins of the law must be expected to reveal moments of low comedy. In a San Francisco case, for example, IRS agents decided to place a pen register on the telephone of a suspect. They installed the device in the telephone terminal box which was in a small room in the building, along with the gas and electric meters. Because there was no other way to lock the door, they placed a hasp and padlock on it. The building watchman, discovering the room was locked, informed the owner. Together they broke through the door, found the pen register, and promptly called the police who put the room under surveillance. Later, when the IRS agents returned, they spotted the police stake-out and posted a man to watch *them*. Eventually the police left, at which time the agents removed the pen register and decamped.

The Subcommittee learned of a case in Boston in which IRS agents admitted to having used practically every form of snooping. This was started as a routine audit and tax investigation, but some time later it was reclassified under the Organized Crime Drive.

The principal suspect, Bernard McGarry, was in the tavern, liquor, and cigarette business. From an observation post in a barn owned by McGarry's next-door neighbor, IRS agents using binoculars watched McGarry's wife sunbathing. Later, she left the house and, in her absence, an agent entered the empty house and examined a vault in the cellar. It contained clothing. The agent noted from a label the name of Mrs. McGarry's furrier, and from the label on a sport jacket, "Leighton's Clothing."

The aim of this stake-out was ostensibly to learn who visited the McGarrys in the evening. This was done by listing the license numbers on the cars that came and went. To help make the list, the agents borrowed a sniperscope from the Army. This is an infrared device designed to permit the user to see in the dark. The first time it was tried, the sniperscope did not work. The second time, it worked but not well enough to read the numerals on license plates.

On one occasion, McGarry was tailed to a mailbox where he deposited a large manila envelope. IRS agents went to the box to check the time of the next pickup. It was their intention to return then and have the mailman show them the envelope. While at the box, one agent coincidently deposited a post card, and discovered, on pulling down the slot, that the McGarry envelope had failed to drop into the box. Without touching the envelope, he was able to read the address on it. The letter was addressed to McGarry's son who was attending school in Philadelphia. An IRS agent was dispatched to talk to him there, and to follow up the "Leighton's Clothing" lead in New York.

Despite the admission of one agent that he had obtained this lead by entering the McGarry home, the other agents denied any knowledge of any such act on his part. However, they were unable to explain where this particular lead came from.

In this case, along with other snooping techniques, IRS had placed mail covers on McGarry, and obtained from the telephone company the records of his long-distance calls. Further, an agent went to his bank and reviewed all his bank records. This review was conducted without the agent's having served the bank officials with an administrative summons. The Subcommittee found that many banks open their depositors' records to IRS agents automatically and never inform the depositor that an investigation has been made.

IRS agents found themselves in hot water with the Federal District Court over one aspect of this same McGarry case. Three agents had gone to the home of McGarry's accountant and alerted him to the fact that the investigation of his client had now become a criminal matter. They proceeded to examine McGarry's books, and then served a summons on the accountant for them. The books were then carted away. The Federal District Court was petitioned to order return of the books, and it did so. It also directed that no use be made of information found in them, since they had been seized illegally. When the IRS agents returned the records, their office kept copies of them that it had made. The copies were ultimately returned, but only after the Federal Court ordered the IRS agents to show why they should not be cited for contempt.

With so many night riders abroad in the land, they are

bound to step on each other's heels on occasion. In one case, an IRS agent, playing golf one day at a Miami links, returned to his car to discover an FBI man searching his trunk.

Less amusing and considerably more obnoxious was the Kansas City case in which local police worked with IRS to place a transmitter in a suspect's apartment. Entry into the apartment was made in a clearly unconstitutional manner, the owner of the building using his passkey. He also planted the bug under the victim's divan while the IRS agents acted as lookouts. The bug was serviced and removed in the same way it was installed. In this case, there were at least three illegal entries in addition to recordings of the suspect's conversations in his home.

Other Agencies: The Subcommittee hearings brought out questionable activities by a number of other agencies. In one case, in 1960, the Immigration and Naturalization Service placed an attorney under such close physical surveillance that one of his clients could not contact him. Here, an alien had been summarily deported without an opportunity to seek *habeas corpus.* He had reentered illegally and was trying, through the attorney, to arrange for his surrender to the authorities under circumstances that would permit him to obtain bail while regularizing his status. Agents placed such close watch on the attorney that the alien could not get near him without risking immediate arrest. On one occasion, they obtained the lawyer's car keys from the attendant at a summer resort parking lot, so that he could not leave without first talking with them.

Another case concerned the Agency for International Development. It was found that, as part of our foreign aid program, we had been furnishing electronic surveillance equipment to other nations. Thus, the nation that had stood for so many years as an international symbol of the rights of man was now producing privacy-invasion devices for export. The Director of AID had not known of this, and he immediately ordered a halt to these activities when the Subcommittee brought them to his attention.

The Senate Subcommittee on Administrative Practice and Procedure has been criticized for its investigation of the IRS, particularly as it relates to the Organized Crime Drive. The IRS argument is that its illegal acts have been few, and resulted from excessive zeal on the part of individual agents who were "continually exposed to the flouting of law, the bribery of public officials, the intimidation of citizens, the defrauding of the revenues, and the full use —by the criminal element—of all the techniques of modern science and communication." It has countercharged that the Subcommittee hearings have had a bad effect on vigorous law enforcement, but these allegations lose substance in the face of the Revenue Service's lengthy and tarnished record.

Two employee organizations closely related to the subject of the hearings have expressed strong support for the Senate Subcommittee's efforts. The Communications Workers of America and the National Association of Internal Revenue Employees have, by resolution, endorsed the Subcommittee's declared intention to put an end to wiretapping and bugging.

The Senate Subcommittee's investigations have led to a number of immediate corrective actions other than those already mentioned. On June 17, 1965, IRS Commissioner

Cohen issued a directive stating that illegal searches and seizures were taboo. The directive also reaffirmed the earlier regulation that illegal wiretapping would not be tolerated, and that electronic equipment was not to be used except with the approval of a designated official of the Service. It further stated that, normally, approval for such use would be given "only in cases involving (1) violations of public trust by Service employees, (2) the attempted bribery or corruption of Service employees, or (3) suspected or known members of the criminal element." To substantiate the validity of Commissioner Cohen's directive, it was reported to the Senate Subcommittee in both Miami and San Francisco that some of their electronic equipment had been returned to the regional or to the national office. Commissioner Cohen also advised the Subcommittee that no more IRS agents would be sent to the Treasury Department's snooping school until it revised its curriculum by dropping the more objectionable subjects.

As for the Treasury Department, on August 5, 1965, a directive was issued to its various enforcement agencies in which wiretapping is again prohibited, except with the consent of one party to the conversation. The only exception is in national security cases. Bugging is also banned, except with the consent of one party to the conversation, but this ban would not apply in areas where bugging is lawful under court decisions. In all circumstances, use of taps or bugs now requires prior approval of supervisory personnel, unless all parties to a conversation consent to the use of a listening device.

Reports have also come to the Subcommittee that U.S. Attorneys in various states have, in light of the information brought out at the hearings, instructed the heads of all federal law-enforcement agencies in their states to obey the federal ban on wiretapping, and strictly limit their use of bugging devices.

In the course of its hearings throughout the country, the Senate Subcommittee on Administrative Practice and Procedure heard a consistent and disturbing story from IRS agents: Despite the fact that some individual states have laws expressly forbidding wiretapping, each agent testified that he had learned of the state ban in his own locality only immediately prior to the Subcommittee's appearance in that area. It may be pleasant to think how enlightening the airing of such problems can be on both sides of the hearing table; nonetheless, citizens in a free society have cause for concern that this kind of calculated ignorance is so widespread in any federal agency.

On July 15, 1965, White House Press Secretary Bill D. Moyers made this statement:

> I know that the President feels that what the Senate Committee is doing is in the public interest and that it is doing a service to the country. . . .
>
> I remember at some of the first conversations he had . . . early in his Administration, he expressed his position that wiretapping, other than that related to the national security, is not consistent with the best traditions of the country.
>
> He has issued instructions to members of the Cabinet and to agency heads concerning what the position of this Government is regarding wiretapping. He has said, very simply, that wiretapping must be related to the security of the Nation, and approved by the Attorney General. . . .
>
> Three or four weeks ago he made a rather vigorous state-

> ment to members of the Cabinet and to agency heads and departments setting this position forward. He said he recognized that from time to time interfering with conversations in this regard, using mechanical and electronic devices may be essential in protecting national security but it must not be condoned or tolerated under other circumstances.

Holding true to form for controls in this area, the instructions of the President were construed differently by the various federal agencies. The Treasury Department, as noted above, merely tightened control over bugging while the Justice Department understood the President to mean that bugging was subject to the same strict limitations as wiretapping. In a memorandum filed with the Supreme Court in the Black case in 1966, the Department said "Present Departmental practice, adopted in July, 1965, in conformity with the policies declared by the President on June 30, 1965, for the *entire* [italics added] federal establishment, prohibits the use of listening devices (as well as the interception of telephone and other wire communications) in all instances other than those involving the collection of intelligence affecting the national security. The specific authorization of the Attorney General must be obtained in each instance when this exception is involved." Apparently the Treasury Department is in that 10 per cent that never gets the word.

7

The Supreme Court and "Dirty Business"

During our nation's first century, searches and seizures were physical in nature and therefore clearly visible to the naked judicial eye. But wiretapping and other technological advances have introduced subtle, complicating elements. Formerly, searches could not be made without entry, while now it is possible to seize and preserve even such intangibles as speech.

The application of the Fourth Amendment to these modern techniques of search and seizure has caused many problems, and the Supreme Court has often felt it necessary to look elsewhere to decide the wiretap and bugging cases that have come before it. As a result, the federal law protecting citizens against electronic snooping by government agents has been clarified only in certain specific areas; outside these, there is almost total anarchy. In fact, Attorney General Nicholas Katzenbach has said that "it would be difficult to devise a law more totally unsatisfactory."

The fault, however, does not lie principally with the

Court. Congress and the Executive must share the blame, with primary responsibility for the present state of affairs resting squarely on the Executive.

In 1927, the Supreme Court agreed to review the question of whether the use of wiretap evidence violated the Fourth and Fifth Amendments. The case, *Olmstead* vs. *United States,* was one in which the defendants had been convicted for conspiring to violate the Volstead (or Prohibition) Act. Federal agents had tapped and monitored the Olmstead telephones for several months. The defense contended that the tapping was contrary to the Fourth Amendment, and the use of the wiretap evidence was contrary to the self-incrimination clause of the Fifth Amendment. By a vote of five to four, the Court found neither amendment applicable.

The majority opinion presented a review of earlier cases which had construed these amendments. It paid particular attention to *Boyd* vs. *United States* and *Weeks* vs. *United States.* In the first, the Court had held that the government could not force the production of private papers for use as evidence against their owner in a criminal trial. In the second, the Court had held that the government could not use as evidence objects obtained by unreasonable search and seizure. The opinion noted that, since the defendants had not been compelled to speak over the tapped telephones, there was "no room for applying the Fifth Amendment unless the Fourth Amendment was first violated." In resolving this question, the Court found wiretapping involved no physical intrusion or trespass into a home or office, and no seizure of material things. In the words of the Court: "The evidence was secured by . . . the sense of hearing and that only. There was no entry of the houses. . . . The language of the Amendment cannot be extended and expanded to include telephone wires reaching to the whole world from the defendant's house or office."

The Fourth Amendment gives protection to a letter in the mail, but the Court refused to apply this principle to a telephone call. For one thing, it found that, a letter was a piece of paper, a material and tangible thing, and a telephone conversation was not.

It was in his dissent in this case that Justice Oliver Wendell Holmes made his often-quoted reference to wiretapping as a "dirty business." He did not base his opinion on the Fourth Amendment, but felt rather that "Government ought not to use evidence obtained and obtainable only by a criminal act," and "for my part I think it a less evil that some criminals should escape than that the Government should play an ignoble part." The federal agents had violated state law when they tapped the defendants' telephones.

On the same occasion, Justice Louis Brandeis argued that wiretapping *was* subject to the Fourth Amendment, and he joined Justice Holmes in opposing the use of evidence obtained by a criminal act. The Brandeis dissent (quoted in part on p. 101) is a basic text for those who view wiretapping as subject to the Fourth Amendment.

The Supreme Court has never re-examined its decision in the Olmstead case with reference to wiretapping. As a result, with one very limited exception, wiretapping remains today an acceptable law-enforcement practice as far as the United States Constitution is concerned.

The exception was defined in the Judith Coplon case.

After the New York pretrial hearing which, as has been noted, revealed extensive wiretapping, the defendant's Washington conviction was challenged on the grounds that her conversations with her attorney had been tapped. This, it was claimed, denied her the effective aid of counsel guaranteed by the Constitution. The District of Columbia Court of Appeals upheld this claim, and returned the case to the trial court for a hearing to determine if there had been such client–attorney interceptions. If so, the Court directed that a new trial be granted. The hearing was never held. While this decision applies only in the District of Columbia, it is reasonable to assume that the same point would be made by courts elsewhere throughout the country.

Nearly seven years after Olmstead, in 1934, Congress enacted the Federal Communications Act. Section 605 of the Act provides that

> no person not being authorized by the sender shall intercept any communication and divulge or publish the existence, content, substance, purport, effect, or meaning of such intercepted communication to any person; . . . and no person, having received such intercepted communication or having become acquainted with the contents, substance, purport, effect or meaning of the same or any part thereof, knowing such information was so obtained, shall . . . use the same or any information therein contained for his own benefit or for the benefit of another not entitled thereto.

The Act provides criminal penalties, and since the adoption of this law, all federal wiretap cases coming before the Supreme Court have been decided on the basis of its provisions.

The Federal Communications Act was a comprehensive measure designed to bring order into the field of radio and wire communications. Wiretapping was not one of its original targets. In fact, there was no mention of the practice on the floor of Congress during consideration of this legislation. But it was not long before the applicability of Section 605 to wiretapping became apparent. Soon cases were making their way into the Supreme Court, their attorneys carrying the statute like a banner. All of these cases were concerned with the statute's application to *government* wiretapping. By the end of 1939, the protection of Section 605 against government privacy invasion had reached its outer limits. Since then, all cases, with one exception, have tended to limit the scope of Section 605. As these are landmark cases in the history of American individual freedom, they are worth examination. The first such case was *Nardone* vs. *United States.*

In this case, federal agents had tapped the defendants' telephones. At the trial, they testified concerning interstate calls they had monitored. The defendants were convicted for smuggling and concealing alcohol. Before the Supreme Court, the government argued that Congress did not intend Section 605 to prohibit tapping wires by law-enforcement officers to procure evidence. The Court dealt roughly with this, however: ". . . the plain words of Section 605 forbid anyone, unless authorized by the sender, to intercept a telephone message, and direct in equally clear language that '*no person*' shall divulge or publish the message or its substance to '*any person*' [italics added]. To recite the contents of the message in testimony before a court is to divulge the message." The Court held the wiretap evidence inadmissible, reversed the convictions, and returned the case to the trial court.

The government quickly brought the defendants into court again, this time introducing no wiretap evidence, and they were once more convicted. During the trial, the defense asked to examine the prosecution as to any use it might have made of information obtained from the taps, but the trial court would not allow this. On appeal before the Supreme Court in 1939, the convictions were again reversed. This time the Court held that, where the government had wiretapped, the defense has a right to determine what use, if any, has been made of the information in the trial. In the Court's judgment, *Section 605 prohibits the use in federal court of evidence derived from wiretap leads* [italics added], as well as wiretap evidence itself. The Court made the point that facts obtained by wiretapping do not become sacred and inaccessible. If knowledge of such facts may be obtained by means other than wiretapping, their truth may be proved like that of any other fact.

On the same day the second Nardone case was decided, the Court decided *Weiss* vs. *United States,* a fraud case which also involved Section 605. Here, federal agents had intercepted telephone conversations that were intrastate, rather than interstate as in Nardone. Also, the wiretap testimony in the Weiss case was presented by participants in the intercepted calls, rather than by the agents. Before the trial, these participants had been confronted by U.S. attorneys with the wiretap evidence, and persuaded to turn state's evidence. At the trial, they gave testimony concerning telephone conversations in which they had taken part. All defendants were convicted, and they appealed.

Before the Supreme Court, intrastate calls were held liable to the protection of Section 605. As to divulgences authorized by the sender, the Court said: "The Act contemplates voluntary consent and not enforced agreement to publication. The parties were ignorant of the interception of the messages and did not consent thereto. The [wiretap evidence] prior to the trial [was] made available to Government agents and . . . attorneys. This divulgence was not consented to by either of the parties to any of the telephone conversations." The Court reversed the convictions by a unanimous decision, and returned the case to the trial court.

The government was not ready to quit. One of the defendants in the Weiss case had taken no part in the intercepted calls, so the government retried him and he was convicted. Once more the witnesses who had turned state's evidence gave testimony, but this time none of it was concerned with the intercepted telephone calls.

Deciding this (*Goldstein* vs. *United States*) case some four months after Pearl Harbor, the Supreme Court now upheld the conviction. Justice Roberts explained why the wind had changed: ". . . even though the use made of communications by the prosecuting officers to induce the parties to them to testify were held a violation of statute, this would not render the testimony so procured inadmissible against a person not party to the message. This is the settled common-law rule. There was no use at the trial of the intercepted communications, or of any information they contained as such."

Federal wiretapping did not stop but federal prosecutors, for the most part, stopped trying to use wiretap evidence in federal court. It was reasonably clear that, while the Supreme Court might bend a little, as in the Goldstein case, it was firmly against the use of wiretap evidence or evidence derived from wiretaps. Fifteen years were to pass before it again reviewed a federal case involving Section 605.

On December 9, 1957, the Court decided two cases in which wiretap evidence had been used to secure federal convictions. In the first, *Rathbun* vs. *United States,* the Pueblo, Colorado, police, at the request of a man named Sparks, had listened in on a regularly installed extension phone in his home, and overheard a threat to Sparks' life spoken by Rathbun. The Supreme Court upheld the use of the police testimony at the trial. Chief Justice Warren, writing for the Court, said, "Each party to a telephone conversation takes the risk that the other party may have an extension telephone and may allow another to overhear the conversation. When such takes place, there has been no violation of any privacy of which the parties may complain. Consequently, one element of Section 605, interception, has not occurred."

This decision has served as a small boon to law-enforcement officers. Although the Court emphasized that a regularly installed extension telephone had been used in Rathbun, the decision has been viewed by some officials as permission to tap with the knowledge and consent of one party to a conversation.

The other related decision of 1957, *Benanti* vs. *United States,* was one in which New York policemen, on the trail of a suspected dealer in narcotics, had obtained a court order to tap the telephone in a bar. As a result of this tap, they were able to seize not narcotics but cans of alcohol without tax stamps. Benanti was then tried in federal court on the alcohol tax violation, and the New York police testified at the trial as to the role of the wiretap. He was convicted, and he appealed.

Before the Supreme Court, the government advanced two points to support its earlier admission of the wiretap evidence: (1) the tap was used without the participation or knowledge of the federal government, and (2) Congress did not intend Section 605 to prohibit taps specifically authorized by state law. The Court rejected both arguments. Lack of federal participation in the tap made no difference, the Court ruled, because *divulgence* of wiretap evidence is specifically prohibited. As to the second point: "We find that Congress . . . did not mean to allow state legislation which would contradict that [prohibition]." Benanti's conviction was reversed.

The decision made it clear that, despite state laws authorizing wiretapping and the use of wiretap evidence in state courts, a federal crime would be committed whenever there was divulgence of such material. Actually, the Supreme Court had said the same thing five years earlier, in *Schwartz* vs. *Texas,* but in that case there had been no state law specifically authorizing police wiretaps. The Court had upheld the use of wiretap evidence in a state court, saying that even though the presentation of this evidence was a federal crime, it was up to the state to determine whether it should be admitted.

The federal wiretap law, as it applies to the states, can be summarized as follows:

It is illegal for state and local police to tap wires *and*

divulge evidence that has been so obtained even under state laws that specifically authorize tapping. But there is no federal check or balance available to prevent the state from using the results obtained from its illegal action. As to how the law applied to the federal government, two professors, Edwin J. Bradley and James E. Hogan, summarized it in one sentence in the Georgetown Law Journal in 1958: "On timely motion by a defendant who was a party to the call, a federal court will suppress the contents and evidence derived therefrom, of any interstate or intrastate telephone communication overheard by any person, whether a private citizen or federal or state agent, if the listening in is without the permission of the other party to the call."

Despite the efforts of the Supreme Court to give real meaning to Section 605 as a protector of privacy, the Justice Department virtually nullified its efficacy in 1941. The Supreme Court has never had an opportunity to do anything about it, and the Congress has never taken an opportunity to do anything about it. Section 605 refers to both interception and divulgence, but the Court, while dealing with divulgence, has never been called upon to determine if wiretapping interception alone is illegal. Many eminent jurists have stated that it is, but this question has never been decisively resolved, and their statements have therefore not been legally binding.

In March, 1940, Attorney General Jackson had banned wiretapping in the Justice Department, as a result of the two Nardone decisions and the Weiss decision, plus the refusal of Congress to amend Section 605. Under the law and the decisions, the Attorney General announced that he had no other choice. But by May, the war in Europe was going badly, and the President had directed limited use of wiretaps when authorized by the Attorney General and where necessary for the defense of the nation. An effort to obtain Congressional approval of wiretapping had again failed. So the Attorney General found himself in the awkward position of approving FBI wiretaps which, according to his announcement, were illegal. But the use of the word "and" between "intercept" and "divulge," in Section 605 (see p. 131), offered him an escape.

In 1941, Attorney General Jackson pointed out to Congress that "There is no Federal statute that prohibits or punishes wiretapping alone. . . . Any person, with no risk or penalty, may tap telephone wires and eavesdrop . . . and act upon what he hears or make use of it that does not involve divulging or publication." Significantly, the statement overlooked the last part of Section 605 which forbids the use of wiretap information, and this myopia on the part of the Justice Department still exists today. With the foregoing statement, Jackson sounded the death knell for Section 605, not only as a protection against government wiretapping but as a shield against private tapping as well.

By 1942, the Justice Department was concentrating its attention on the issue of divulgence. The problem was how to explain persuasively that divulgence of wiretap information between federal agents and agencies was not the same as the divulgence referred to in the statute. The Justice policy accepted the line that all government agencies formed a single entity. Thus, divulgence within the government was not the same as divulgence to the general public, the divulgence allegedly contemplated by the statute. This was the final nail in Section 605's coffin.

Twenty years later, Francis Biddle, who had been Attorney General in 1942, was asked by a Senate committee why the Justice Department had never tested its own construction of Section 605 in the courts. His answer was a practical one: ". . . I should think that the Department felt that they were getting what they wanted, the information they wanted . . . although it did handicap them not to be able to disclose it in court. . . . I am pragmatic about these things, and if I think a thing is first rate, I don't go into court to have it suggested that it is illegal."

So, while the Supreme Court has given Section 605 a stature almost equal to the Fourth Amendment, the Justice Department, which still follows the convenient Jackson-1941 construction, has reduced it to no more than a rule of evidence. The protection afforded by 605 is further reduced by the secret nature of wiretaps: the victim seldom knows that a tap is (or has been) in operation and, therefore, cannot invoke the protection of the law at the time it is needed.

The Department's construction has opened the field to wiretapping by state and local law-enforcement officers. Private operators are also tapping under this hypertechnical interpretation of the law. The Justice Department has never brought a prosecution, in the case of law-enforcement tappers, even where state officers have divulged wiretap evidence in state court, nor has it ever brought a case based on wiretapping alone. And, if one remembers the Biddle statement in extenuation of the pragmatic approach, one can see why. Under the present construction, the Department is doing well enough, so why rock the boat?

Several states have adopted their own wiretap laws and

this causes additional confusion. Some of these statutes aim to protect the privacy of telephone calls, while others merely protect the property of the telephone company. Some prohibit all wiretapping, while others prohibit only the private variety. Some require the police to obtain court orders to tap, while others allow them to tap whenever the urge seizes them. In some states, courts have found constitutional objections to wiretapping, and in others neither the courts nor the legislatures have dealt with the subject of police tapping.

There is one point on which all states seem at least tacitly to agree: regardless of the legal situation, little is done to prevent tapping. As a result, in this area we have the worst possible legal situation for a free society: not only is there legal confusion on both state and federal levels, but there is intentional disregard of the law by government agents, and failure to meet enforcement responsibilities under the law. On occasion, law-enforcement agencies will try to justify their policies on wiretapping, but the facts speak much more convincingly for themselves.

As a widely used snooping technique, bugging came to maturity more slowly than wiretapping. This was because bugging presented certain practical problems not met in wiretapping. To bug a room, one had to have access to it, and this was not always so easily arranged. But modern technology has, as we know, come to the snooper's rescue. It has provided him with a number of ways to monitor conversations without actually having to secrete a device in the room where the conversations take place. It has also provided devices that can be installed more quickly and with less fuss than the earlier bugs.

Wiretapping deals with telephones and thus can be tied to interstate commerce, but bugging is a strictly local activity. There is, for this reason, some question as to the authority of Congress to control bugging directly. In any case, it has enacted no specific legislation regarding bugging. This lack of rules has worsened an already thoroughly confused situation.

The first bugging case came before the Supreme Court in 1942. This was *Goldman* vs. *United States,* having to do with a violation of the Bankruptcy Act. Federal agents, by means of a detectaphone placed against the outside wall, had monitored the defendant's conversations in his office, including some on the telephone. The Supreme Court saw nothing wrong in this under the law. It found that Section 605 did not cover snooping on one end of a telephone conversation but was intended, rather, to protect conversations in the process of transmission. As to the Fourth Amendment, the Court held that, since the detectaphone was merely placed against the wall in the adjoining office, there had been no trespass and it could find no distinction between this case and Olmstead.

Ten years later, the Court handed down another milestone decision in *On Lee* vs. *United States.* This was a narcotics case. Evidence was secured by fitting out an old friend and former employee of the defendant with a small transmitter hidden inside his coat, after which he engaged On Lee, who owned a laundry in Hoboken, in an incriminating conversation. The conversation was, of course, monitored by federal agents planted with a receiver outside the laundry.

Again the Court threw out the protection of Section 605, this time because "There was no interference with any communications facility which [the defendant] possessed or was entitled to use." As to the Fourth Amendment, the false friend with the hidden transmitter had not trespassed, but had entered On Lee's establishment with the victim's consent. And without trespass, there could be no unreasonable search and seizure.*

This was a hairline decision with five affirmations and four dissenters. Justice Frankfurter filed a vigorous dissenting opinion, saying, in part, "The law of this Court ought not to be open to the just charge of having been dictated by the 'odious doctrine,' as Justice Brandeis called it, that the end justifies reprehensible means."

Two years later, in *Irvine* vs. *California,* the Court gave warning that the Fourth Amendment might apply to bugging, if there was trespass, even though only intangible words were seized. In this case, the police had secretly planted a microphone in the Irvine home, first in a hallway and later in the bedroom. Here is what Justice Jackson said, speaking for the Court: "That officers of the law would break and enter a home, secrete such a device, even in a bedroom, and listen to the conversation of the occupants for over a month would be almost incredible if it were not admitted. Few police measures have come to our attention that more flagrantly, deliberately, and persistently

* The Court's verdict, however, included the following warning: "The use of informers, accessories, accomplices, false friends, or any other betrayals which are 'dirty business' may raise serious questions of credibility. . . ."

violated the fundamental principles declared by the Fourth Amendment." Despite these sharp words, Irvine's conviction was upheld because, under the governing cases at the time, evidence obtained in violation of the Fourth Amendment could be used in state courts.

In 1961, in *Silverman* vs. *United States,* the Supreme Court at last held the Amendment applicable to one form of electronic snooping. This was a case in which the District of Columbia police, investigating a gambling operation, had driven a spike mike from an adjoining apartment into the defendants' wall. The spike made contact with the heating system of Silverman's house and thus it became, in effect, a giant microphone. The overheard conversations were used in evidence, and the defendants were convicted in the local federal courts.

The Supreme Court again found no "interception" under Section 605 since only one end of the defendants' telephone conversations had been overheard by the police. But, the Court ruled, "Eavesdropping accomplished by means of such a physical intrusion is beyond the pale" of previous examples which had come before the Court. And ". . . the Fourth Amendment, and the personal rights which it secures, have a long history. At the very core stands the right of a man to retreat into his own home and there be free from unreasonable governmental intrusion. . . . But decision here does not turn upon the technicality of a trespass upon a party wall as a matter of local law. It is based upon the reality of an actual intrusion into a constitutionally protected area. . . ." The Supreme Court reversed the convictions.

In a similar case in 1964, *Clinton* vs. *Virginia,* the Supreme Court threw out a state court conviction based on evidence obtained by use of a small spiked listening device that had penetrated the wall between the defendant's apartment and the one occupied by police.

On May 27, 1963, the Supreme Court decided another milestone case, this one, *Lopez* vs. *United States.* Here, a federal agent had used a small hidden recorder to register a bribe offer, and the recording had been used in evidence. The Court this time affirmed the conviction on the ground that there had been no "eavesdropping." "Instead, the device was used only to obtain the most reliable evidence possible of a conversation in which the Government's own agent was a participant and which that agent was fully entitled to disclose."

There were three dissenters in this case and they were chiefly concerned with the effects of electronic devices on freedom of speech. For all those who cherish the democratic heritage, the view of Justice William Brennan strongly warned: "I believe that there is grave danger of chilling all private, free, and unconstrained communication if secret recordings, turned over to law-enforcement officers by one party to a conversation, are competent evidence of any self-incriminating statements the speaker may have made. In a free society, people ought not to have to watch their every word so carefully."

While Congress has not enacted laws specifically related to bugging, a federal regulation does exist that is applicable to bugging with transmitters. The Federal Communications Commission has regulated radio broadcasting for many years. Except for transmitters which operate within a small exempt area as to frequency, power, and length of antennas, such devices must be licensed. Unless a snooper uses a licensed transmitter, or one that falls within the exempt area, he is liable to prosecution under Section 502 of the Federal Communications Act. Several persons in the District of Columbia were so prosecuted as a result of a bug planted in the Mayflower Hotel in 1962. This was the first effort to control bugging at the federal level.

On February 25, 1966, the FCC directed new regulations specifically against eavesdropping. It prohibited, except for law-enforcement agencies, the use of any radio device to overhear or record the private conversations of others without the consent of all persons involved in the conversations. Again, prosecution would follow from Section 502. The regulation applies to all types and sizes of transmitter, licensed or not, and to the use of them at any point in an eavesdropping scheme. If a conversation is held where it is reasonable to expect that others may overhear it, it is not protected by the regulation. There was an exemption also for transmitters used by enforcement officers acting under lawful authority. But the Commission indicated that, if this exemption proved unwise, it would look into the issue further and revise the regulations.

Despite the loopholes, these regulations represent a major step forward in protecting privacy. They outlaw a broad area of private snooping. It should be noted that, in taking this action, the FCC in no way reduced its requirements as to licensing, and police and other eavesdroppers must still comply with these regulations.

This is the confused and often conflicting record of the federal law today on electronic snooping techniques. The use of these techniques is an aid to law enforcement, but this same use raises profound constitutional questions. Despite this obvious conflict, neither Congress nor the courts have made the necessary frontal assault on the issue. Congress appears willing to rest content with Section 605, secure in the knowledge that law enforcement is getting just about what it wants. The courts, on the other hand, have been unable to resolve the knotty problem of physical intrusion. As a result, they have been forced to cast around for other means than the Fourth Amendment to protect privacy from electronic snooping.

At this point, another portion of Justice Brennan's dissent in the Lopez case is highly appropriate: "Electronic aids add a wholly new dimension to eavesdropping. They make it more penetrating, more indiscriminate, more truly obnoxious to a free society. [They make] the police omniscient; and police omniscience is one of the most effective tools of tyranny. . . . I cannot but believe that if we continue to condone electronic surveillance by federal agents by permitting the fruits to be used in evidence in the federal courts, we shall be contributing to a climate of official lawlessness and conceding the helplessness of the Constitution and this Court to protect rights 'fundamental to a free society.' "

8

Congress and the Invasion of Privacy

SINCE THE 1928 OLMSTEAD DECISION, wiretap bills have been introduced in every Congress except the Seventy-fourth (1935–36) and the Seventy-ninth (1945–46). Over these years almost one hundred bills have been marched up the hill, and over a dozen hearings held. From the Olmstead to the Nardone I case, the bills were aimed at outlawing wiretapping but since Nardone, they have been aimed at legalizing some law-enforcement wiretapping.

Congressional concern about the issue actually began some years prior to the Olmstead case. When the federal government took control of the nation's telephone and telegraph systems during World War I, Congress felt a double responsibility—to protect the privacy of communications and the property of the private owners. In 1918, it prohibited wiretapping or other interference with the systems or their operation. This law died when the systems were returned to private hands at the end of the war.

After this, wiretapping remained a dormant issue until the Olmstead decision. Then, in 1929, Representative

Robert H. Clancy introduced a bill to prohibit it. Shortly after, Representative John C. Schafer introduced another such bill and, in the same year, Representative George Tinkham interrogated J. Edgar Hoover as to the wiretap policy of the Bureau of Investigation. Director Hoover told the House subcommittee that he thought it "unethical" and that its use was "not permitted under the regulations by the Attorney General."

A year later, Representative Tinkham was aiming his questions at Colonel Amos W. W. Woodcock, Director of the U. S. Bureau of Prohibition. Colonel Woodcock interpreted the Olmstead decision as giving his agency a free hand to wiretap. His position was no surprise, since it was well known that Prohibition agents tapped wires.

Early in 1931, Tinkham offered an amendment to an appropriations bill that would have banned the use of any funds for the tapping of telephone or telegraph wires in the enforcement of Prohibition. The amendment was defeated. Early in 1932, three new bills were introduced into Congress to do something about wiretapping and Representative Tinkham had a chance to interrogate the Attorney General.

Again, no official action was taken.

In that year, the controversy over Prohibition was reaching its peak, and the debate over funds for the Bureau was highly colored by personal attitudes toward the Prohibition law. Here again a wiretap amendment was quashed. Early the next year, Tinkham was finally able to attach a wiretap amendment to a bill appropriating funds for the Prohibition Bureau. There was a certain irony in the timing of this bill's success, however. The day the Senate approved it, it also approved the amendment that repealed Prohibition.

It was only one year after Tinkham's moral victory that the Congress approved the Federal Communications Act with its provision against wiretapping. The wiretap issue was then permitted to rest in Congress until the Nardone decision in 1937.

Congress reacted swiftly to the Nardone decision. Within three months, Senator Burton K. Wheeler introduced a bill that would have permitted heads of executive departments to authorize wiretapping in certain cases, and would have allowed admission of the evidence so obtained in federal court. The bill never got out of Congress.

This bill, which before being permitted to die had passed both the Senate and the House, was as close as Congress has ever come to authorizing law-enforcement wiretapping. Senator Wheeler, the committee chairman who handled it originally, changed his mind about it after he had looked at it more closely. When it returned from the House with an amendment, he refused to call it up for Senate concurrence.

The first move in Congress after the second Nardone decision and the Weiss decision, was not new legislation to permit tapping but rather a Senate Interstate Commerce Committee resolution, in March, 1940, which called for an investigation of wiretapping and certain other devices. The Committee report, filed by Senator Wheeler, spoke of "the recent resurgence of a spy system conducted by Government police. Persons who have committed no crime, but whose economic and political views and activities may be obnoxious to the present incumbents of law-enforcement offices, are being investigated and cataloged. . . ."

The ensuing hearings revealed, among other things, that a private investigator, working with the Governor of Rhode Island and a special assistant state attorney general, had tapped the telephones of the state's Attorney General, and the Mayor of Pawtucket, Rhode Island. Also a Philadelphia hotel room had been bugged. Despite the inevitable protestations of public necessity, the testimony left little question that the tapping was actually done for political purposes.

The hearings also revealed wiretapping in New York and Washington, D.C., exposing a spiderweb of snooping operations by private investigators. On the list of alleged victims of these attentions were J. Pierpont Morgan, the Guaranty Trust Company, John W. Davis, the Amtorg Trading Company, and Justices of the U.S. Supreme Court.

The day on which the Senate opened these hearings was, by coincidence, the same day (May 21, 1940) on which President Roosevelt wrote the confidential memorandum to Attorney General Jackson, directing him to tap where necessary for the nation's defense.

Soon after, Congressman Celler introduced a bill to permit law-enforcement wiretapping. It was passed by the House but died in a Senate committee.

In January, 1941, Congressman Hobbs introduced a wiretap bill drafted by the Justice Department. In the course of hearings on this one, several witnesses quoted public statements against wiretapping made over the years by FBI Director Hoover. He answered with a written statement:

"These short quotations . . . must . . . be construed in the light of circumstances under which they were made. I have always been, and am now, opposed to uncontrolled and unrestrained wiretapping by law-enforcement officers. Moreover, I have always been, and am now opposed to the use of wiretapping . . . except for crimes of the most serious character. . . . In . . . espionage, sabotage, kidnapping, and extortion, wire tapping as an investigative function is of considerable importance."

While this was going on, the President was writing to Representative Thomas Eliot: "Dear Tom: I have your letter of February 20th in which you have asked me for . . . my views on . . . a bill to permit wire tapping by Government officials. . . . I have no hesitation in saying that it [the Justice Department bill] goes entirely too far. . . . As an instrument for oppression of free citizens, I can think of none worse than indiscriminate wire tapping. . . ." The President went on to recommend its use in espionage, sabotage, kidnapping, and extortion cases.

James L. Fly, Chairman of the FCC, opposed the bill. He argued that wiretapping would hinder rather than help the national defense program. He also felt there would be no way to control the abuses of wiretapping by law-enforcement officers.

The result of all this activity? Nothing. The bill was defeated on the House floor.

Shortly after the attack on Pearl Harbor, Representative Celler tried once more to put through a bill that would permit wiretapping in national security matters. Despite statements by the Attorney General and others that federal agents were already wiretapping, the following argument was put forward in the House report on the bill: "The restrictions that now obtain against so-called wiretapping have been dangerous bars against effective counterespionage. We have the very anomalous situation wherein enemy spies, saboteurs, and espionage agents flout the restrictions concerning wiretapping which Federal officers rigidly observe. Such a situation is woefully ridiculous."

Four days after this report was filed, the Supreme Court handed down its decisions in the Goldman and Goldstein cases. The proposed Celler bill was then revised so it would authorize only the use of wiretap evidence. It would thus constitute a Congressional endorsement of the Attorney General's position that wiretapping in itself was already permissible under the law.

The measure was passed by voice vote in the House, but it was quickly done to death in the Senate: it never lived long enough to get out of the Interstate Commerce Committee. Despite the urgency of the war atmosphere, the pro-wiretap forces had been unable to put through their bill.

In 1948, the Cold War had replaced the hot war, and the snoopers' army began to move again. In January, a pro-wiretap bill limited to overseas communications was introduced by Senator Alexander Wiley, and, in time, found a burial place in the Judiciary Committee of the Senate. Several wiretap bills were introduced in the House in 1949, but all remained blocked in committee.

December, 1950, saw the reversal of Judith Coplon's New York conviction, and this brought an immediate reaction in Congress. Several new wiretap bills were introduced. One, presented by Representative Celler, was drafted by the Justice Department. All these bills were shunted into oblivion despite the concern over the reversal in the Coplon case.

In August, 1951, a new element, crackling with high voltage publicity, made its appearance. This was the report of Senator Kefauver's "Crime Committee." The committee reported that, in its view, federal agents are handicapped by the unclear legal restrictions that hedge wiretapping. It recommended laws to permit tapping with court authorization and adequate safeguards. But no bill was introduced to carry out the recommendation.

While the Korean War dragged on, concern for our internal security was reflected through many hearings and investigations. Superimposed on the issue now was the provocative political personality of Senator Joseph McCarthy. Another factor adding potent charges to the emotional atmosphere in which the Eighty-third Congress convened was the fresh memory of convicted Soviet spies.

On the opening day of the Congress, January 3, 1953, several wiretap bills were put in the hopper. The ensuing hearings and debate were the most complete exploration of the issue up to that time. Despite the emotionalism that tinged the air, many members of Congress took a serious look at the basic issues.

The Administration's bill dealt only with the use of wiretap evidence in court, and was limited to national security cases. It would authorize the use in court of such evidence obtained both before and after its enactment, provided the Attorney General had approved the tap. It relied on the traditional Justice Department construction as to the legality of the tap itself.

Except for the American Civil Liberties Union, none of the witnesses at the House hearings opposed wiretap legislation. The question was not whether a bill should be enacted but rather what kind of bill it should be. A subcommittee modified and then approved a bill supported by Representative Kenneth Keating. It would permit tapping in national defense cases on court order. But before the bill was reported by the full committee, it was further modified to strike out the need for court orders. Representative Keating supported this change. This was the bill that Majority Leader Charles Halleck dubbed "the anti-traitor bill," and this labeling of the bill became an issue in itself.

Representative Thomas Dodd, a former member of the FBI, addressed himself to this point: "I deeply resent the efforts to pressure and intimidate the Members of the House with respect to this legislation by giving to this proposal the nickname 'anti-traitor bill.' Is it intended that those who oppose this bill are to be called pro-traitor? . . ."

Representative Celler hit out even harder: The label, he said, was "an appeal to sensation, not sanity. It is an appeal to passion, not patience. It is an appeal to fear and frenzy and not frankness. Calling the bill an anti-traitor bill is a shocking revelation of sterility of mind. . . ."

After thorough debate, the House passed the bill with an amendment restoring court orders for future taps. Meanwhile, considerable vocal opposition to law-enforcement wiretapping had been making itself heard. In addition to the ACLU, the Americans for Democratic Action and the Friends Committee on National Legislation sent representatives to the Senate to testify against all wiretapping. The CIO and the American Jewish Congress filed written statements in opposition to it.

After the Senate concluded its hearings, no further action was taken on any of the proposed wiretap bills, including the House-passed measure.

Neither branch of Congress has debated a wiretap bill since 1954, but the issue has remained an active one. In 1958, the Senate conducted hearings on wiretapping, eavesdropping and the Bill of Rights, to bring out the latest thinking on the constitutional issues involved. A two-thousand page record was printed.

Wiretap bills of one kind and another continued to be introduced by members of Congress, but nothing came of them. Then, shortly after the second session of the Eighty-seventh Congress convened in 1962, Attorney General Kennedy sent Congress an Administration wiretap bill. It sought to authorize wiretapping in national security cases on the express approval of the Attorney General, to authorize federal tapping in certain crimes with court orders, and to permit state tapping in certain crimes under state court order statutes. Hearings were held in both Senate and House but the bill failed to move past this stage.

In September, 1963, the nation watched and listened in absorbed fascination as Joseph Valachi told a Senate subcommittee all about his career as a working member in the underworld of crime. The purpose of these hearings was to obtain for law-enforcement officers additional tools—including wiretap—for the fight against organized crime. Despite the drama of these particular hearings, and an appeal from the Attorney General and other witnesses for wiretap legislation, nothing was done.

While Congress has directed its attention mainly to wiretaps in which neither party knows of the presence of the tapper, in 1961 it took a long look at a familiar listening–in practice: government telephone monitoring.

The practice was initiated by the Army Signal Corps in 1938. The first recording devices were installed at the War Department, where they were controlled by switchboard operators who recorded incoming toll calls. At first, all callers were informed that their conversations were being recorded. But by 1940, the recorders were installed on individual telephones and the warning to persons calling the Department was discontinued. The practice continued until after World War II, and by then two thousand such devices had been made available to the War Department. On July 12, 1946, the original rule was reinstituted and no recordings were made unless the other party was notified that it was being done.

It was in that year that the FCC decided to look into the widespread use of such recording. It found that some nineteen thousand such devices were then in use throughout the country, and that about a third of these were the property of the War and Navy departments. The Commission issued an order directing telephone companies to provide a monitoring service, but with certain provisos. One condition was the use of the beep tone that signifies the conversation is being recorded.

The 1961 Congressional inquiry included a survey of fifty-seven federal agencies. This survey revealed that the government was using three types of devices to monitor: the transmitter cut-off, listening–in circuits, and recorders. The first two devices required a third person to listen in on the conversation. The government was, it seems, heavily entrenched in the party-line business. In Washington alone rent on these devices amounted to $30,000 a year.

The final report on the inquiry recommended that each agency adopt regulations to control monitoring, and that provision be made requiring specific notice be given to callers. Of the forty-eight agencies that had regulations by this time, only thirty-three required advance notice to the caller that his every word on the telephone was, in effect, official.

Congressional interest in agency use of secret recording devices was not new in 1961. Two years earlier, the Senate had become concerned over the widespread use of the Minifon, the small, compact wire recorder that can be carried in a shoulder holster under an ordinary suit coat. Even the Department of Health, Education, and Welfare, it was discovered, kept no less than forty-eight of them busy.

Jurisdictional problems have prevented Congress from serious consideration of many techniques that ride roughshod over privacy. But in recent years, the increased use of certain practices, by the government as well as by private persons, has provoked Congressional inquiries.

Special concern has arisen from the psychological testing of school children and government employees. Federal funds have been used to support such testing of school children, and many persons have been bothered by some of the questions that appear on the tests. Parental consent is not always obtained for such tests and, even when it is, parents are often not aware of the nature of the questions to be asked. A school child will not, as a rule, hesitate to answer a question put to it on a test given by an adult, and there is little doubt in the minds of persons who have studied the issue that many of these questions constitute improper invasions of privacy.

In 1965, Congressional hearings revealed that government employees, too, were being subjected to this kind of mind-probing, at the risk of losing their jobs. No one questions the value of such tests in therapeutic situations, but there is considerable doubt of their validity in determining an applicant's fitness for a job. Aside from the matter of propriety, what relevance is there between efficiency in a work situation and questions about sex, religion, family relationships, and other personal matters?

Then, there is the polygraph. Throughout history, man has sought simple methods to determine guilt or innocence. In trial by ordeal, a suspected wrongdoer had to put his hand into a fire or walk on red-hot coals. If unsinged, he was declared innocent. Otherwise, he was obviously guilty. We have no statistics on the number of innocent people who died because they were not immune to fire.

The early Chinese were less brutal. The suspect chewed rice powder while being questioned. If the powder was dry when spat out after interrogation, the man was condemned, since the tension of guilt had presumably dried up his salivary glands. One other reported technique required the suspect to enter a darkened cave and pull the tail of a donkey that had been placed inside. The suspect was informed in advance that the donkey would bray when a guilty person pulled his tail. He was not told, however, that the tail had been painted with lampblack. When the suspect emerged from the cave, if he had clean hands he was considered guilty. It was assumed that only the guilty would be afraid to pull the tail, after all these preparations. This technique had at least the virtue of seeming to be logical.

The polygraph ("lie-detector") test may be more valid than these earlier trials in determining guilt or innocence, and then again it may not. It is based on the idea that an identifiable and identical physical reaction results from a specific emotional stimulus, an idea that is not actually new. Cesare Lombroso, the great Italian doctor and criminologist, claimed, around the turn of the century, relative success in determining the guilt or innocence of suspects by following their blood pressure and pulse rates during interrogation.

The polygraph did not gain wide acceptance until recent years, when our society has learned to depend on the machine for just about everything. With no conclusive data or documentation to support its accuracy, it has been foisted upon business and government to the extent that between 200,000 and 300,000 tests are conducted annually. But our courts have been less easily sold on the merits of the so-called lie detector, and a majority of judges refuses to admit the results of such tests in either criminal or civil proceedings.

A recent Congressional survey exposed the fact that nineteen federal agencies use the polygraph or similar lie-detection devices. There were more than five hundred of these dubious machines working away for the government at an annual operating cost of well over $4 million, including salaries. The lie detector itself costs from $600 to $2,000.

In March, 1965, a House report recorded this measured verdict. "There is no 'lie-detector,' neither machine nor human. People have been deceived by a myth that a metal box in the hands of an investigator can detect truth or falsehood." The report points out that the polygraph "records physical responses which may or may not be connected with an emotional reaction—and that reaction may or may not be related to guilt or innocence." It should also be noted that even though the polygraph operator is the most important human factor in the use of this technique because he frames the questions and interprets the graph, the government has no uniform criteria for the selection of operators, and the training provided is inconsistent and usually inadequate.

Partly because of lax administrative controls, polygraph tests are all too often used in trivial matters. Two-way mirrors and hidden microphones are often used for surveillance during the administrating of these tests. To insure that he will approach the test with the clearest of consciences, the subject is sometimes called upon to divulge incriminating actions completely unrelated to the matter under investigation.

All agencies have claimed that taking the tests is voluntary, but this is straining the meaning of the word. When someone refuses to take the test, the fact is noted in the official files. Also, people with long memories will recall that much of the cooperation provided the Nazis by their victims was also called "voluntary."

As a result of its findings, a House subcommittee urged research to determine the reliability of such tests. It called for their use in only the most serious cases. It further urged that the tests be made truly voluntary, and that the use of two-way mirrors and concealed mikes be restricted. It recommended further that operators be better trained and qualified for their jobs. It was suggested that a Presidential committee should study the problems raised by use of the polygraph in government and work out solutions.

The polygraph's chief stumbling block in the past has been the fact that it cannot always evaluate lies. This is not the best recommendation for a foolproof lie-detector. But people—some of them quite important people—continue to have faith in it. This derives from the general blind spot of our time: a tendency to view the machine, any machine, as infallible. As a result of this entrenched attitude, many opponents of the use of the polygraph have shifted the weight of their argument to the machine's infringement on the right of privacy and the individual's right against self-incrimination.

The struggle in Congress over the use of privacy-invading techniques will continue. The marketplace is glutted with ever more ingenious techniques for depriving the citizen of his right to be let alone—and these techniques are being used by men who are, in many cases, on the payroll of the taxpayer. The battle between individual liberty on the one hand and law enforcement on the other must somehow be resolved.

9

The Role of the States

WIRETAP EVIDENCE obtained in compliance with the New York court order statute had been used in 1957, in the Benanti case, a federal prosecution in federal court. The Supreme Court held, in its decision on the appeal, that it was immaterial that the wiretaps had been placed under authority of state law. Section 605 was violated when such evidence was used in court.

One result of this decision was that District Attorney Edward Silver, of Brooklyn, made the ominous prophecy that "unless Congress does something about this problem soon, they will witness a gigantic legal jail break. . . . Many more who can be indicted won't be indicted."

Under usual circumstances, the Benanti decision would have had little effect on law enforcement in New York, because the Supreme Court had held earlier, in *Schwartz* vs. *Texas,* that states could determine whether wiretap evidence was admissible in their own courts, even though divulgence of such evidence would violate Section 605. For many years, New York courts had admitted illegally obtained evidence. But less than a month after the Benanti decision, a New York judge who had long questioned the value of law-enforcement wiretapping issued an opinion that stated he would no longer grant wiretap orders. Judge Samuel Hofstadter said: "Under the decision . . . in *United States* vs. *Benanti* . . . orders authorizing interceptions are contrary to controlling federal law. Its authority requires me, therefore, to deny any application for such an order. For all wiretaps, whether 'authorized' or not, in this state are now illegal. . . ."

Shortly after this, other judges in New York gave rough treatment to indictments based on wiretap evidence obtained with a court order. In one case, the defendant unsuccessfully sought an injunction in federal court to restrain the Bronx District Attorney and the Police Commissioner from using wiretap evidence in his forthcoming trial. A federal judge felt compelled, in this case, to make an important point: "Normally, it is not the province of a member of the federal judiciary to suggest to a United States District Attorney how he should perform his duties. I point out that in oral argument . . . appellees [the state] did not deny that it was planned to offer wiretap evidence at the trial, and thereby did not deny to five federal judges in open court an intent to commit a federal crime. If such a crime is committed and remains unprosecuted . . . there will have been a most extraordinary affront to this court. Accordingly, I ask that the United States District Attorney for the Southern District of New York follow the proceedings in *People* vs. *Pugach* with the closest attention."

The request for the injunction against the Bronx District Attorney went as high as the U.S. Supreme Court, where, interestingly enough, it was denied. Also interesting is the fact that no New York law-enforcement official has ever been prosecuted for a violation of Section 605. Despite all the highly publicized cries of dismay which continued after each post-Benanti event, most of the alarm on the part of New York law-enforcement officials has been quietly put to rest.

During the furor, however, many New York officials launched an all-out effort to have Congress change Section 605 to legalize state wiretapping with court orders. At the 1962 Senate wiretap hearings, no less than twelve New Yorkers testified before the Judiciary Committee. Between 1958 and 1962, public statements from New York concerning the gravity of the situation were cited continuously.

Six months after the ominous prediction of District Attorney Silver, Manhattan District Attorney Frank Hogan was sending an assistant into court to announce the abandonment of seven narcotics prosecutions. The defendants, he said, were "guilty beyond any doubt," but the key evidence against them had been obtained by wiretaps. To stir up more support for this campaign, Silver composed an imaginary telephone conversation that he circulated widely. He argued that his literary effort represented what would happen under the law after the Benanti decision. Silver's "conversation," ostensibly between a mobster, Peanuts, and his boss, made it appear that laws against wiretap evidence left the door wide open for criminality. A typical section reads:

The Boss: What do you mean "50 horse?" I was expecting 50 kilos of heroin. Give it to me straight.

Peanuts: Gee, Boss, dats no way to talk on the phone, you warned me y'self. I—

The Boss: Listen, dope, that's old stuff. My mouthpiece told me the bulls ain't allowed to stick their snoots in our private business. It's against the law, y'hear? It's dirty business to do such a thing.

Silver was disturbed over the opposition of the American Civil Liberties Union (which, in his "conversation," he renames the Criminal Liberties Union) to his wiretapping crusade. He said: " 'Do gooders,' individuals and groups, have made every effort to confuse the public that this is a problem of civil liberties. Nothing could be further from the truth. Indeed, the New York State Association of District Attorneys has introduced more legislation to protect the rights of defendants than the Civil Liberties Union or any Bar Association. . . . There are so-called liberals who have recklessly, and perhaps willfully, conjured up dire consequences that would result from the power to tap wires with a court order."

One of the main shortcomings of the campaign to "liberalize" Section 605 was the inability of the pro-wiretap New Yorkers to enlist widespread support from the other states. During the 1962 Senate wiretap hearings, there were only eleven witnesses from states other than New York who spoke in favor of state law-enforcement wiretapping. Of the eleven, five were from states that prohibited all wiretapping.

An even more significant reflection of national opinion was provided by a Senate subcommittee a year earlier.

It sent letters to the Attorneys General of all fifty states, asking each one's opinion as to the need for federal legislation on electronic snooping. Forty-five responses were received. *Only thirteen called for laws that would permit state law-enforcement wiretapping.* Twenty-six offered no opinion, and six flatly opposed wiretapping. The fact that twenty-six offered no comment must be considered in light of the circumstance that some states admit illegally obtained evidence and that in these, Section 605 may not pose a substantial problem. It is significant that less than a third of those polled indicated support for legislation explicitly permitting the government-agency wiretap.

Law-enforcement officers tend to be staunch advocates of wiretapping, so why is there this difference of opinion on the state attorney general level? It is probably due to the fact that the attorney general's office is usually a policy-making position, tending to reflect the attitudes of the particular state legislature and courts. By 1962, when the U.S. Attorney General requested a combined federal-state wiretap law, all fifty states had legislation protecting wire communication systems. Thirty-nine prohibited wiretapping, but five of these—New York, Massachusetts, Maryland, Nevada, and Oregon—had court-order systems to allow law-enforcement wiretapping. Louisiana exempted law-enforcement officers from its wiretap ban, while three states—Illinois, Pennsylvania, and Wisconsin—specifically banned such "official" wiretapping. Four states—California, Florida, Michigan, and New Jersey—considered their wiretap laws (by court decision) to apply to law-enforcement officers as well as to the general public, and one, Texas, had not prohibited wiretapping but, on the basis of

Section 605, had denied the use of evidence so obtained in court. In almost half the states, the law prohibiting wiretapping is so worded, or so placed in the statute book, that it appears to be aimed at protecting telephone *property* rather than telephone *privacy*.

There has been wide divergence in state laws since the first was passed by California, in 1862, to discourage tapping of telegraph wires. This is because each state, in its own good time and under conditions that happened to prevail in its own domain, has dealt with the problem in its own way. The body of state law on this issue has continued to grow in patch-work fashion.

In 1938, New York decided to meet the problem of law-enforcement wiretapping. In that year, the state's Eighth Constitutional Convention was called to draft a new state constitution. At the time, New York was the only state that did not have in its constitution a provision equivalent to the Fourth Amendment.

Search and seizure proposals were introduced at the Convention, and Governor Herbert Lehman expressed the "strong belief that a provision should be included . . . which will safeguard each citizen against unreasonable searches and seizures of his home, business premises, papers and effects and that will also protect each citizen against wiretapping of his telephone conversations and telegraph messages, except under order of court. In order to make such a provision effective, the State Constitution should definitely require that any evidence obtained in violation of the constitutional guarantee shall not be admissible in any judicial or other proceedings."

A different view, read into the record, was expressed by

Thomas E. Dewey. He had no objection to including an unreasonable search-and-seizure provision in the law. But he attacked the provisions relating to wiretapping and the use of illegally obtained evidence. In his view, the evidence provision would "protect no one except the guilty criminal. . . . It is designed for the exclusive purpose of depriving the people of this state of evidence of crime. . . . The proposal will have the single effect of protecting murderers, gangsters, and kidnapers. . . ." The wiretap provisions, he felt, would "abolish one of the best methods available for uprooting certain types of crime. . . . During the seven years in which I have been a public prosecutor in New York, I have never known a single case in which wiretaps were used without the overwhelming corroboration by other evidence, nor have I ever seen a single instance where the police in the tapping of criminals' telephones have exceeded proper limits."

The provision eventually adopted by the Eighth Constitutional Convention and approved by the people of New York established a court-order wiretap system, but it did not prohibit the use of illegally obtained evidence in court. Four years after this, the New York legislature enacted a statute that established procedures for obtaining wiretap court orders. And it was approximately two decades later that this court-order system clashed with Section 605 in the Benanti case.

Despite New York's leadership, other states continued to ignore the issue of law-enforcement wiretapping. Then, in the 1950's, many legislatures began to come to grips with the problem. Between 1953 and 1958, at least fifteen states considered legislation ranging from court-order measures to total bans. Texas led the way. In 1953, in response to the Schwartz case, that state prohibited the use of wiretap evidence in court.

In the Schwartz case, the Supreme Court had held that the use of wiretap evidence was a federal crime, but it had left it up to the states to determine whether information obtained by tapping should be admitted under such circumstances. Unlike New York in 1958, the Texas Legislature did not call on Congress to change Section 605. Instead, it changed its own law. Such constructive reaction to a Supreme Court decision is, indeed, unusual.

In 1955, Oregon adopted a court-order system. Maryland and Nevada later followed suit. Pennsylvania and Illinois, however, enacted total bans. Even after the Benanti decision made it clear that states could not legalize wiretapping, state legislatures continued to wrestle with the issue. Wisconsin reinforced the federal law by enacting a total ban, but Massachusetts instituted a court-order system.

State action to resolve the conflict between the needs of the state and the rights of the individual has by no means stilled unrest. The Benanti decision prevents state court-order systems from operating effectively. As an example, District Attorney Frank Hogan, of New York, has not requested a wiretap order since Benanti, nor has he used wiretap evidence. From states that ban wiretapping completely, voices continue to be heard asking for wiretap authority. As time passes, more states will decide the wiretap question one way or another, but so long as we have crime and telephones (or technological advances in communications) the controversy will continue.

States and local police, like their federal counterparts,

have often followed policies of their own devising, carefully disregarding the policies set by legislatures and courts. In California, for instance, the statutory ban on wiretapping applies, by court decision, to the police as well as to everyone else. Yet Samuel Dash, in his book, *The Eavesdroppers,* wrote in 1959 that, despite this ban, wiretapping was used by local police. He reported that, since district attorneys and police departments could not show wiretapping equipment in their budgets, they had adopted the device of hiring private specialists. In the same year, however, Mr. Dash told a Senate subcommittee that he had found no evidence of alleged police wiretapping in Los Angeles since 1950.

In one California case, local police used a complete array of electronic surveillance devices. A Hollywood fight promoter had reported to the Los Angeles police that he was a victim of an extortion scheme being carried out by gangster Frankie Carbo. With the promoter's consent, the police placed an induction coil and recorder on his phone, and a bug in his office. They also equipped the promoter with a transmitter when he met with a representative of Carbo. In the resulting federal prosecution, the use of all tapes was upheld by the Ninth Circuit Court of Appeals.

On the basis of the record, it would appear that, today, law-enforcement wiretapping is fairly well controlled in California. The practice is largely limited to situations in which the police have the consent of one party to the conversation.

Florida, too, has a wiretap ban which is supposed to apply to the police as well. Yet a Senate subcommittee was told by a Dade County electronics expert, in 1965, that he had installed wiretaps during his service with the Sheriff's department. He said, however, that in each case it was done with the consent of the party whose telephone was tapped. In some of these cases, he had placed taps for federal agencies.

As far as wiretapping is concerned, no state has had as much experience as New York. There is a good deal of disagreement as to how much of this tapping has been done by law-enforcement officers. The statistics presented by official sources show a restrained use of the practice. According to these data, the number of court-order taps runs to less than 1,500 in a normal year. Alan Westin, Professor of Government at Columbia University and a prominent expert on the subject, told a Senate subcommittee, in 1958, "I think there has been evidence that there has been, particularly at the police department level, a good deal of wiretapping without obtaining court orders." A year later, the same subcommittee was told by Samuel Dash that his observations led him to believe that the New York police operated at least 13,000 taps a year, and possibly twice that number.

In wiretap hearings before the House Judiciary Subcommittee in 1955, one witness, William Keating provided testimony of unusual interest on New York law-enforcement officials at work. Mr. Keating had been counsel for the New York City Anti-Crime Committee and, before that, a member of District Attorney Hogan's staff. He testified specifically concerning abuses of the New York court-order system. He told of one situation, while he was on the District Attorney's staff, in which a court order had been obtained to tap the phone of one of the city's best-known political figures. Allegedly, the order had been obtained in connection with a murder investigation, but in fact the murderers had been convicted six months before the order was requested.

Keating also told of a waterfront investigation, in 1939 or 1940, in which many wiretap orders were drawn on different telephones in different investigations, but the same case name was used on all applications for the orders. It was clear from the testimony that most New York courts relied on the judgment of the specific District Attorney, and seldom requested any information other than the bare recitations contained in the application. This point has been made frequently by law-enforcement officials and New York judges.

New York officials who support their court-order system admit the persistence of illegal police tapping. In 1950, a Brooklyn grand jury investigating a notorious underworld figure revealed that armies of plainclothes policemen were installing wiretaps virtually at will. Sometimes they were doing this with fraudulently obtained court orders, but more often they had no orders at all. Perhaps in tribute to the concept of free enterprise, many plainclothesmen had provided their own wiretapping equipment. Miles F. McDonald, District Attorney of Brooklyn, gave a bleak picture of this problem to a House subcommittee in 1953: "We found . . . in the Gross case . . . that police officers without instructions were buying their own wiretapping equipment. They would sit in on a telephone such as a coin booth near a baseball park or near a race track, and when they heard people call up to make a bet, they would forward that to another plainclothes detective who would then go and shake that bookmaker down. But that was all unauthorized wiretapping."

New York's wiretap procedures were tightened after this case. In 1955, the state legislature looked into electronic eavesdropping, and the first report of the investigating committee referred to police wiretapping under procedures then in effect as "a secretive, hole-in-the-wall operation, somewhat akin to second-story work. It seems to us beneath the dignity of the law and of the processes of the court."

What information there is on wiretapping at the state and local level shows it is being done very frequently. Just how frequently can probably never be determined beyond doubt. Nevertheless, there are enough facts to draw certain conclusions: the total-ban statutes seem to be most effective in achieving protection of privacy, since they deprive the police of any reason to possess wiretap equipment. Also, they leave no room for any justification of a tap.

The New York court-order system has not been effective in controlling law-enforcement wiretapping. Law-enforcement officials in New York City seem to rely much more heavily on wiretapping than do Kansas City officials, for instance, who are subject to no inhibiting state law. And it is not possible to explain the contrast in these approaches satisfactorily by citing any differences in the nature of crime in the two cities.

The legal status of wiretapping seems to have little bearing on crime rates and, to date, there has been little evidence that the difference in wiretap laws has any effect on adequate law enforcement. New York, Boston, and Baltimore, operating with court orders, continue to have crime problems as acute as those in cities where wiretapping is banned. FBI statistics have shown in recent years that New York and Nevada, both court-order states, are among those with the highest crime rates. Pennsylvania and Wisconsin, on the other hand, rank among the states with the lowest crime rate, despite their statutory ban on all wiretapping. None of the states that authorize law-enforcement tapping are among those with the lowest crime rates. It would appear that experience at the state level does not answer many hard questions about wiretapping, but does re-emphasize the threat this practice offers to the privacy and liberty of the individual.

The Benanti decision, recent legislative and judicial actions, and new developments in electronic snooping devices have all tended to shift police activities away from wiretapping. Bugging and various forms of wireless snooping are now favored methods of surveillance. In California, a committee investigating bugging heard one witness testify that he had done electronic snooping at various times for police departments in at least eleven California cities. He also stated that he has worked for a number of sheriffs, district attorneys, the State Medical Board, the State Pharmaceutical Board, and the Narcotics Bureau. Witnesses for the Los Angeles Police Department, Sheriff's office, District Attorney, and State Attorney General's offices, told the committee they possessed sound monitoring equipment and personnel. According to them, bugging had been used in many types of criminal offense such as extortion, abortion, grand larceny, bookmaking, narcotics, and bribery. The Los Angeles District Attorney's office was the only agency offering comprehensive statistics and it reported that, between 1951 and 1955, it had used an average of ten bugs a year, with ninety per cent of them installed with the consent of the occupant of the premises.

Two years prior to this inquiry, the California Supreme Court had severely curtailed police bugging activities. The Los Angeles police, suspecting that a man named Cahan was a bookmaker, had surreptitiously entered a house used by his brother and installed a mike there. Then, posing as exterminator servicemen, they gained access to the home of Cahan's bookkeeper where they planted a second mike. On the basis of evidence obtained by monitoring these installations, the police later raided—without warrants—several places used by Cahan's group, thereby obtaining additional evidence. The state Supreme Court reversed the convictions of these defendants in the lower courts. Its decision pointed out that "without fear of criminal punishment or other discipline, law-enforcement officers, sworn to support the Constitution of the United States and the Constitution of California, frankly admit their deliberate, flagrant acts in violation of both Constitutions and the laws enacted thereunder. It is clearly apparent from their testimony that they casually regard such acts as nothing more than the performance of their ordinary duties for which this city employs and pays them."

The California committee was told by one witness who engaged in electronic snooping full-time that, prior to the Cahan decision, 75 per cent of his work was for public agencies, and 25 per cent for private individuals. After Cahan, the figures were reversed.

New York had had experience with the problem of corrupt policemen indiscriminately using the benefits of surveillance techniques to shake down criminals. Instances of such misuse were cited before the California committee, too. In one case, in Los Angeles, a policeman "had the wires of a suspected vice operator tapped, then attempted to 'shake her down' with the recordings that were made. He was discharged and prosecuted for his undertaking."

As a result of the committee inquiry, there was increased concern over electronic snooping. There was also an awareness that the California police found no insurmountable problem in adapting to the Cahan decision without loss of effectiveness. It is not surprising that the state legislature extended California's antidictagraph law to all electronic eavesdropping and, in effect, removed the exemption that had been previously granted to the police. The statute does, however, permit the use of bugs with the consent of one party to the conversation.

The New York experience is worth looking at in more detail. Sensational newspaper stories of eavesdropping brought the matter to a head in 1955. After an investigation of the situation by a committee of the state legislature, certain suggestions for additional restraints on wiretapping and electronic snooping were forthcoming. Over the next few years, several bills were adopted, some were vetoed by the Governor, and a number of compromise measures became law.

The committee had recommended a court-order system for all snooping, but the Governor twice vetoed such a measure. He also vetoed a recommendation that unlawfully obtained wiretap and eavesdropping evidence be inadmissible in criminal proceedings. The law that was finally adopted in New York did not, for all its admirable intent, close the loopholes in law-enforcement eavesdropping it was originally designed to do. Two incidents came to light a short time later that spurred efforts to tighten the new eavesdropping law.

The first incident was the secret recording in the Westchester County Jail of conversations between "Socks" Lanza, a racketeer, and his lawyer, and between Lanza and his family. The monitoring was done at the request of the Parole Board. The second incident was the revelation that the New York City Transit Authority had for two years been bugging the activities of the Motormen's Benevolent Association, a union to which many of its employees belonged. The bugging had begun shortly after the motormen's union had been formed, in the fall of 1955. The New York police were fully informed that bugging was taking place and, for a long period, received transcripts of of the monitored conversations from the Transit Authority police.

An attempt was made to justify this bugging on the basis of law enforcement. But Anthony P. Savarese, Jr., chairman of the committee that revealed the situation, noted that the bugs had proved to be of no law-enforcement value. Rather, he said, "I conclude that the secret microphones had definite value for the Transit Authority in labor relations, if labor spying can be called that. The entire operation was directed at one group of workers and bears the unwholesome taint of old-world persecution by secret police."

One result of the committee's inquiry was a new bill calling for court orders to bug, but allowing police in an emergency situation to install a bug without such an order.

In such "hot pursuit" cases, however, application for an order must be made within twenty-four hours. This bill became law on July 1, 1958.

New York's efforts to deal with the problems of wiretapping and electronic snooping were followed by many similar struggles in other parts of the country. It was during this period that the four other court-order systems were adopted. When Nevada acted, in 1957, it made court orders necessary not only for wiretapping but also for bugging. Nevada was thus the first state with a court-order system that specifically applied to the latter practice. In addition to these two states, Oregon, Maryland, and Massachusetts have also banned wiretapping and electronic eavesdropping except by court order. But there is one major distinction in these bans: under Oregon and Maryland law, the act is illegal without a court order unless *all* parties consent to a monitoring or recording of their conversation. In the other three states, the consent of only one party is sufficient to proceed. It was during this same period, incidentally, that Illinois put through an unconditional ban on all wiretapping and bugging.

Except for these six states, and California, there appears to be no other state that specifically prohibits private electronic eavesdropping. In some, Peeping Tom statutes and general eavesdropping laws might be interpreted to cover snooping devices, but some states do not have even these laws. In such states, any protection against private bugging would have to be found in the old common-law rule against eavesdropping. A situation in which one would have to rely on this kind of dubious protection would be hardly reassuring.

In 1965, Maryland became the first state to try one further approach to the regulation of tapping and snooping. Its legislature made the manufacture or possession of any wiretapping or eavesdropping device unlawful, unless registered with the State Police. Several other states have adopted labor laws which prohibit acts of surveillance and spying as unfair labor practices that interfere with the rights of employees.

Considering the steady technological advances in this field, it is hard to believe that only seven states have laws prohibiting private use of bugging devices and regulating law-enforcement use. While the wiretapping situation on the state level is bad primarily because of lack of enforcement, it is far better than the bugging situation; at least there exists in most states the threat of possible prosecution of the wiretapper. Also, there is possible federal prosecution under Section 605.

It can be hoped that the new FCC eavesdropping regulations will have an effect on the bugging situation, but at best it can only be limited. The snooping situation today is serious and, if we hope to preserve even a fragment of our rapidly disappearing privacy, action by the states is essential.

In view of recent Supreme Court decisions, the lack of state laws has created a condition that has not only grave implications but a certain perverse humor, as well. In the Silverman case, it will be recalled, the Court held that the use of a spike mike by federal police officers violated the Fourth Amendment, and this decision prevented the use of evidence so obtained in a federal trial. Subsequently, the Court held in *Clinton* vs. *Virginia,* that the same rule applied to state and local police, and to state courts. Thus the Fourth Amendment prohibits all law-enforcement officers from using snooping devices where their installation requires the slightest physical trespass or unauthorized penetration of an area of privacy such as a house, office, or automobile. This means that there are forty-three states in which law-enforcement officers cannot use certain eavesdropping techniques to apprehend law violators that private citizens are free to use for any purpose.

The Court's decision in *Clinton* vs. *Virginia* not only points up the need for state laws to prohibit private bugging, but it also opens the whole question of state law-enforcement bugging. In forty-five states, officers clearly may not eavesdrop where a trespass or penetration is involved, because there is no means for them to obtain a court order or warrant as referred to in the Fourth Amendment. But what about officers in the five states that have court-order systems? Many hold the view that a court order for bugging is tantamount to a search warrant, and meets all the requirements of the Fourth Amendment. These orders, they argue, not only make the snooping legal but make the trespass necessary to install the bug equally legal. A New York judge, in 1965, decided to the contrary.

Judge Nathan Sobel found several constitutional weaknesses in this argument. For one thing, the Fourth Amendment requires that a search warrant *specify* the thing to be seized. Judge Sobel found there is no way to determine in advance what is going to be said. But even if there were, a bug seizes *all* conversation, and there is no way to limit it to specific statements. Thus, a court order for bugging cannot meet the Fourth Amendment demand that it must be specific.

Secondly, the judge found, a warrant can be issued only for certain types of things: fruits of crime, instruments of crime, contraband, and goods upon which duties have not been paid. Warrants cannot be issued for evidence composed of intangible words which would not fit into any of the categories presently subject to a warrant. Because of the inability to be specific, and the very nature of eavesdropping itself, court orders for bugging have the effect of a general warrant. The reader will remember that the general warrant was one of the evils most inveighed against by the men who decided to break with England and fight for American independence.

In the case before Judge Sobel, the state had shown ample probable cause for the court order which it obtained in March, 1963. But the conversations ultimately used by the police were seized four months later: the order was issued to bug a service station because its owner was implicated in a larceny case, but the seized conversations dealt with the possession of firearms.

The judge raised at least three more possible constitutional weaknesses. He concluded that, regardless of whether a court order is obtained or not, the Fourth Amendment is violated when "eavesdropping is effectuated (1) by means of a physical invasion or intrusion, (2) upon a constitutionally protected area."

The decision of Judge Sobel would appear to be sound. To find to the contrary, a court would have to change substantially the meaning the Fourth Amendment has had for over one hundred and seventy-five years.

After the Supreme Court decision in *Mapp* vs. *Ohio,* a suit was brought in federal court to have the New York wiretap court-order system declared unconstitutional. This case eventually went to the Supreme Court. The Court refused to review the decision of lower courts that had denied the petition. It would appear from this that the Supreme Court is not yet ready to re-examine fully the Fourth Amendment issue raised by wiretapping. If it should do so, however, wiretap court orders could find themselves in the same precarious position as those issued for eavesdropping.

Mapp vs. *Ohio* also opened to question other earlier decisions of the Supreme Court in the privacy area. There is, for instance, the case of *Breithaupt* vs. *Abram,* in which a blood sample was taken from the defendant while he was unconscious in the hospital after an accident. The results of the laboratory test were then used in state court to convict him of drunken driving. Here, the U.S. Supreme Court upheld the conviction. It felt that the right to be immune from such invasion of privacy was far outweighed by the need to protect society by use of the most modern methods of crime detection. The taking of a blood sample was found to be a routine medical procedure in a modern hospital, and not offensive to our sense of justice. This particular decision was reconfirmed by the Court just before it closed its term in June, 1966.

At the state level, concern over privacy has not been limited to physical searches, wiretapping, and eavesdropping. A few legislatures have ventured into other areas. In eighteen states, for instance, the information given to a psychologist by a client is now privileged. Seven states have banned the use of "lie detector" tests as a condition of employment, although all these states but one have put limitations on the ban. Since organized labor is campaigning to have the use of such tests barred in employer-personnel situations, it is likely that other states will, in time, enact similar laws.

Most state legislatures, like Congress itself, have failed to keep abreast of advances in the field of privacy invasion. The techniques multiply and become increasingly ingenious, but the states do little or nothing. As to the more obvious techniques of wiretapping and eavesdropping, only a few states have confronted the problem in their legislatures, and fewer still have enforcement policies that provide the protection offered by statute.

There can be little doubt that the controversy over law-enforcement use of privacy-invading techniques will continue. But what is even more certain is that, if some vestige of individual privacy is to be preserved for the average American, adequate laws, both state and federal, must be enacted *and enforced.* And this must happen soon. Otherwise, we may be trapped in a situation in which effective action is no longer possible.

While technology races, legislation crawls.

10

Secrets for Sale: The Eavesdropping Industry

"OUR GOVERNMENT IS THE POTENT, the omnipresent teacher. For good or for ill, it teaches the whole people by its example. Crime is contagious. If the Government becomes a law-breaker, it breeds contempt for law; it invites every man to become a law unto himself; it invites anarchy. To declare that in the administration of the criminal law the end justifies the means—to declare that the Government may commit crimes in order to secure the conviction of a private criminal—would bring terrible retribution." So Justice Brandeis warned in his dissent in the Olmstead case.

Despite the Brandeis warning, this is exactly what has happened in the field of snooping. Outright violation of the law by the federal government has led to anarchy in the investigative field. Because of their own unlawful activities, government officials are reluctant to enforce the law against other violators, many of whom have been taught by their example.

It is true that the Justice Department's construction of

Section 605 gives a semblance of legality to its agents' wiretap activities. But its failure to prosecute vigorously under this strained construction clearly indicates that even the Department recognizes the shakiness of its position. In the more than thirty years since Congress enacted Section 605, less than thirty cases have been brought against private wiretappers, and none have been brought against law-enforcement wiretappers.

The departmental attitude was established as far back as 1940. At that time, Attorney General Jackson directed that his department withdraw from its investigation of the wiretap episode involving the Governor and the Attorney General of Rhode Island. He took this action, the press reported him as saying, because the federal government could not in "good conscience" prosecute wiretappers when it was engaged in the practice itself and, under certain circumstances, regarded it as legal.

A year later, however, the Justice Department brought its first prosecution under Section 605. A New York lawyer, Jacob Gruber, represented a client who was involved in an investigation by the Securities and Exchange Commission. Trying to get advance information on SEC plans for his client, Gruber had enlisted the aid of a telephone operator at the New York office of the Commission. When conversations pertinent to Gruber's client were on the line, the operator arranged to have Gruber listen to them through a conference system. The scheme was discovered, and Gruber was tried and convicted of violating Section 605.

At first glance, this action appears to contradict the earlier statement by Attorney General Jackson. But actually it is safe to assume that, in the Gruber case, the Justice Department was less interested in enforcing Section 605 than it was in preserving the integrity of a federal agency, in this instance, the SEC. Ten years went by before another 605 case was prosecuted. The long lapse of time and the nature of the next case, permit no other judgment but the one already made here as to the nature of the Justice Department's concern.

In 1951, a racing news service whose leased telegraph lines passed through California was barred by state law from furnishing information to people in that state. Casper Rotondo, Sr., and others were convicted for conspiring to tap these lines and furnish the stolen information to California bookmakers. Here again, it seems probable that the government was not especially interested in the enforcement of Section 605, but was primarily concerned with illegal gambling.

Until 1953, a jurisdictional problem had complicated law enforcement of major antisnooping legislation by the Justice Department. The Federal Communications Commission, established by the Communications Act of 1934, was authorized to administer the Act. As a result, there was some question as to whether the FCC or the Justice Department was responsible for enforcement of Section 605.

In October, 1952, Paul A. Walker, Chairman of the FCC, wrote to the Attorney General expressing the view that the Justice Department was responsible for enforcing the troublesome law. This was the fifth effort of the Commission, since 1948, to get the Justice Department to take over such enforcement: four earlier letters had gone unanswered. On January 16, 1953, Attorney General McGranery at last responded to the letter of the previous October. His department, he wrote, was now prepared to assume such responsibility.

The clarification of jurisdictional responsibility has improved the situation somewhat, but not very much. A 1965 report of the Justice Department shows that the pre-1953 average of one case in every ten years has jumped to an average of two cases each year.

Since 1953, about three out of four of the cases brought into court have resulted in convictions, guilty pleas, or pleas of *nolo contendere*. Fines, probation, and suspended sentences have been the rule. More than half the cases have involved private detectives and marital disputes, and the courts have been reluctant in such cases to impose prison terms. Strangely, only one case on the list involved what might be termed industrial espionage.

Today's private wiretapper really has little to worry about from federal enforcers. In the first place, his activities are unlikely to be discovered by the government, but even if they are, the chances that he will be prosecuted are slight. If prosecuted, the likelihood that he will be sent to prison is even more slight. As a result, Section 605 offers little if any deterrent to private wiretapping.

As for the law-enforcement wiretapper, he has less to worry about than his private colleague even if he publicly and blatantly violates the law. Despite Judge Waterman's comment in the Pugach case when he called on the U.S. Attorney to prosecute violations of Section 605 by law-enforcement officials, the Justice Department has held fast to its nonprosecution policy. Why?

In 1960, Brooklyn District Attorney Edward Silver was asked if Attorney General Rogers had expressed himself on this matter. He replied: ". . . in view of the fact, as he says, that Congress has as yet not had an opportunity to express itself, they will not entertain any complaints against law enforcing agencies, be they district attorneys or police."

In 1962, Attorney General Kennedy made it clear that he had not changed this policy. He told the Senate Judiciary Committee: "The Department has been reluctant to prosecute State officials for actions taken in good faith in compliance with State law, in the absence of a clear-cut congressional mandate. . . . The solution, we feel, is for the Congress, in the light of twenty-five years' experience, to establish clear-cut rules and limits which will define, much more precisely than Section 605, exactly what law-enforcement officers can and cannot do. Armed with such clear-cut rules, we can, and I assure you that this administration will, prosecute vigorously anyone who violates them." Kennedy admitted a short time later that "Even though, under applicable State laws, State law-enforcement officers may wiretap, recent Federal court decisions make it clear that the disclosure in court of evidence obtained by such wiretapping is illegal under Section 605." Despite this admission, the nonprosecution policy has not been changed.

A curious example of this official do-nothing policy was offered by Professor Alan Westin, of Columbia University, to the Senate Constitutional Rights Subcommittee in 1961. It concerned an incident that took place in Philadelphia several years before. In Westin's words:

> The then district attorney in Philadelphia, Victor Blank, had put a telephone tap in the hotel room of several labor organizers whom he characterized as labor racketeers and hoodlums who were coming to Philadelphia in order to take over a restaurant union.
>
> The tapes he acquired from the telephone tapping were then given to the newspapers in Philadelphia, and one of the . . . newspapers . . . published verbatim the transcript of the telephone taps.
>
> There was a demand for an investigation by the U.S. Attorney, made by the City Council of Philadelphia, by the local Civil Liberties chapter and by the Philadelphia Bar Association.
>
> At the time the U.S. Attorney in Philadelphia did investigate, and, to my mind, disappointingly, he did not find that there was a ground for prosecution under Section 605.
>
> I would have thought where, in this case, there was no prosecution ever made of the men [labor organizers] who had come and sat in the hotel room and made telephone calls and where the district attorney divulged the information he acquired and published it, gave it to the newspapers for publication, this would have been an ideal case for the Department of Justice to say, "Now, at least in this kind of situation, we are willing to move against police violators of Section 605 as well."

The Justice Department's use of wiretapping and its double standard of enforcement, running from lukewarm efforts against private wiretappers to none at all against law-enforcement wiretappers, has had a disastrous effect on privacy in the United States. Congress and the Supreme Court have done little enough in this area, but even this little has been mostly undone by the attitude of the Justice

Department. In the words of Justice Frankfurter: "The contrast between morality professed by society and immorality practiced on its behalf makes for contempt of law. Respect for law cannot be turned off and on as though it were a hot-water faucet."

Like the federal government, many state governments teach wiretapping and eavesdropping by example. And even where there are adequate laws to prevent the use of these practices, little effort is made to enforce them.

The result has been a free-for-all in the use of sophisticated snooping techniques. Committees of both the New York and the California legislatures concluded that professional eavesdropping in their states was "a lively, active, lucrative private business."

As has been mentioned earlier, a rabbi, a Baptist minister, and the local Director of the American Friends Service Committee in Baton Rouge, Louisiana, were the victims of a wiretapper in 1961. They had been active in promoting racial harmony. In the fall of 1960, when trouble developed over public school desegregation, fifty-three ministers joined in signing an "Affirmation of Religious Principles." It urged the maintenance of the public school system, and called racial discrimination a violation of the divine law of love. The three wiretrap victims were among the signers.

The following March, the Baptist minister suspected that his telephone, or that of his Quaker colleague, was being tapped. There were reports that tape recordings of their telephone conversations were being played before groups in the community. With the help of the telephone company, a tap was discovered on the telephone of the

American Friends Service Committee office. The situation was reported to the U.S. Attorney in New Orleans, and a federal grand jury began an investigation.

In the meantime, the Baptist minister and his family received threatening phone calls at all hours. Because of this and other harassments, the minister resigned his post, and he and his family left Baton Rouge.

As a result of the federal grand jury's inquiry into the case, indictments were returned, under Section 605, against a Louisiana state senator, a private detective, and a Baton Rouge businessman. The detective was charged with intercepting telephone conversations, and the other two men were charged with divulging the contents of such conversations, knowing them to have been obtained by wiretapping.

A small but significant epilogue to this case occurred in a CBS television interview with the Baptist minister. He described his feelings during subsequent visits to the city where he and his family had been hounded and their privacy invaded: "I have a strange and ominous feeling on each visit here—walking down the street, or riding in an automobile, and most particularly in talking on the telephone, I really have difficulty in bringing myself to speak clearly and openly about whatever might be at hand. I always have the feeling that I am still not alone when I'm in Baton Rouge."

There have been few clearer personal statements of what happens to the average individual when his right to privacy is systematically invaded.

The largest and most fantastic wiretap operation of all time was discovered in New York City in 1955. The New

York Telephone Company received an anonymous tip that something was wrong at its exchange located at 56th Street and Third Avenue, and that illegal wiretapping was being conducted there. This led to the discovery of an operation that had been in existence for over a year.

The taps were installed at the main frame of one of the busiest telephone exchanges in the world. A cable ran from the exchange to the plant, which was located in a fourth-floor apartment on East 55th Street and which contained ten automatic recording machines. The grid monitored at the plant included some 60,000 telephones within a twenty-five block area. The number of people at work in the wiretapping operation was small: two telephone company employees, an electrician, and a private investigator.

The story of what happened after the original anonymous tip attests once more to the benign attitude of most telephone companies and law-enforcement officials toward private wiretapping. After the tip, the company began an investigation, and two employees soon came under suspicion. The taps were traced to the headquarters on 55th Street and two special agents of the telephone company, along with two city detectives, went to the apartment there and knocked on the door. Before answering, the tapper in residence—it was the electrician—disconnected all recorders from the cable and turned off all machines. According to him, he was asked in the course of the raid if the equipment was his, but none of the raiders seemed curious enough to ask if he had actually been wiretapping.

After an hour or so, the four visitors left the apartment without making an arrest or confiscating the equipment. They pursued this hands-off policy despite the fact that, under New York law, possession of such equipment—not to mention private wiretapping—is a crime. The man who had played host to the quartet of raiders claimed that one of them, especially considerate, had told him before leaving to get rid of the equipment because the four would return the next day. After the raiders left, the electrician immediately erased all the tapes on the machines.

Later in the day, the two implicated telephone company employees were interrogated by the company and suspended. The company would not sign a complaint, however, because at the time of the raid on the apartment the recorders had not been connected to the cable leading to the exchange.

Apparently this was to be the end of the matter. But about five or six days later, word of the raid was leaked to the New York City Anti-Crime Committee. This was a private agency similar to other citizen crime commissions and it had been pressing for a state investigation of wiretapping. It immediately brought the information it had received to the attention of the New York State Legislature, and also released it to the newspapers. The front-page publicity that resulted changed the course of events. The New York County District Attorney immediately began an investigation of the 55th Street operation. Neither he nor the Police Commissioner had been informed of the raid. An example of the theatrical effects to be found in a wiretap case is provided by the wistful complaint of the District Attorney: the equipment from the fourth-floor apartment was now missing and he could not find out where it was.

The two telephone company employees and the electrician were indicted, and pleaded guilty to conspiracy and illegal wiretapping. The chief executive of the operation, private investigator John G. Broady, was indicted on twenty counts of conspiracy, illegal tapping, unlawful possession of wiretap equipment, and unlawful use of premises for wiretapping.

The 55th Street plant, it developed, had tapped the telephones of many well-known companies and persons. Among these were the St. Joseph Lead Company, the Knoedler Art Galleries, the chairman of the board of Pepsi-Cola, a television actress, a former burlesque star, a chemical manufacturer, a prominent lawyer, and a publishing company. It had also monitored the conversations of many people with presumably private marital problems.

In the trial, it was brought out that Broady had received $60,000 from Charles Pfizer & Company, a large pharmaceutical house, for his services. In October, 1954, an attorney who did legal work for Pfizer took Broady to see the company's general counsel, who outlined problems that Pfizer was having with security. He also told Broady of litigation the Pfizer Company was engaged in, including a patent problem involving Bristol-Myers and concerned with tetracycline.

According to trial testimony, Broady was asked to check the telephones at various Pfizer offices for wiretaps. He was also to check the company's conference rooms for hidden microphones, and the home telephones of certain company officers as well. He was to do this without alerting Pfizer personnel that a security investigation was under way.

Subsequently, the general counsel and Broady met about once a week at the entrance to the Holland Tunnel. At the second such meeting, Broady was given a list of about fifty employees and asked to check their living standards, the people they associated with, their work habits, and related matters. It was indicated then that the list might be expanded to three hundred names.

But the general counsel soon found that he had not the time to go through the detailed reports Broady began to submit. Broady was then asked to confine his reports to the highlights of what the investigation was revealing. In the midst of this, Broady arranged to have a tap installed on the New York office of the Bristol-Myers Company, as well as a tap on the direct line to its main office in Syracuse. Because the E. R. Squibb Company was also involved in the tetracycline situation, Broady arranged to tap the phones of that company. To help him in this matter, the employee he shared with the telephone company obtained a list of all outside-line telephones at Squibb.

Chief target of these taps, which were begun around Christmas, was the private line of a Squibb vice president. One of the monitored conversations disclosed the number of a second private line, and another tap was promptly made on it. These taps continued until the raid.

According to the testimony at Broady's trial, the accused told his tapping colleagues that the Squibb taps were a security check installed at the behest of Squibb itself. But he gave no explanation for the Bristol-Myers taps. Pfizer's general counsel denied having received any reports from Broady concerning taps on either Bristol-Myers or Squibb, and Broady himself denied ordering either the Bristol-Myers or the Squibb tap. Something of a virtuoso at denials, he denied ordering any of the wiretaps covered by the indictment, and he also denied having the electrician lease the apartment on 55th Street.

He was sentenced to two to four years in jail and on appeal the Supreme Court refused to review his case.

The public disclosure of this carnival of wiretapping in 1955 led the New York Legislature to establish the Joint Legislative Committee to Study Illegal Interception of Communications. This Committee soon recognized that it would be impossible to take a census of the wiretappers in New York, so it decided to concentrate on one known and presumably typical wiretapper and his activities. Broady was ruled out because of the criminal action pending against him. It chose as its subject a private investigator, Charles V. Gris, who had been licensed to operate in New York for thirteen years.

In the course of its hearing in New York City, the Committee heard from many witnesses, including clients and employees of Gris. In one of the cases, most of which involved marital disputes, one of the taps was discovered by the telephone company and the tapper was identified as a Gris employee. The latter was interviewed by the company but, in keeping with its sixty-year policy of extreme courtesy in such matters, no complaint was made to the police.

The majority stockholder of the Hazel Bishop Company told of hiring Gris to check the telephones of company officials because of suspicions aroused by the revelation of matters that had been discussed *only* over the telephone. With the aid of a telephone company employee who figured in the Broady case, Gris discovered taps on the phones of several Hazel Bishop officials. Presumably these taps had been producing information for Hazel Bishop competitors over a period of eighteen months. At almost the same time that the Committee was told of the telephone company employee's discovery of the Hazel Bishop wiretaps, the same employee testified in court that he himself had installed a tap on Hazel Bishop's line six months before he was hired to check the company's lines. Here is a case of "double agent" snooping—the tapper searching out his own tap!

Another witness was the comptroller of Revlon. He told the Committee that Revlon had had its own telephones monitored for five or six years by the telephone company. He maintained that this had greatly improved employee performance and had created higher morale. He also testified that in April, 1955, arrangements were made to have Gris and the telephone company employee tap the office telephone of one Revlon worker for security reasons.

The Committee was interested also in learning how and where Gris obtained his electronic equipment. One device had been procured from a Connecticut manufacturer who professed to sell only to law-enforcement officials. Gris had purchased the item in the name of the West New York, New Jersey, police.

One of the witnesses was sufficiently interesting to provoke these special comments in the Committee's 1956 report: "Bernard Spindel . . . represents a contradiction in terms, a publicity-loving practitioner of a surreptitious occupation. Through newspaper interviews, newspaper and magazine articles, and testimony before a committee of Congress, he has celebrated his own prowess and skill at 'electronic eavesdropping.' It appears established that Spindel gave the New York City Anti-Crime Committee its first information about Broady's wiretapping nest. In a number of instances, Spindel gave this Committee leads which assisted it in its inquiry. . . . Spindel boasts of many successful microphone installations, and freely admits many 'legal' wiretaps. In all this he holds himself forth as a proponent of civic virtue and the enemy of unlawful wiretappers. His legal distinctions have not impressed the ethical sensibilities of the Committee. We believe all eavesdropping is bad and should be punished as a crime."

In 1958, Gris, who was once convicted for violating Section 605, was indicted along with three others, under New York's new eavesdropping statute, for installing a secret microphone. After the indictment was returned, he committed suicide.

Ten years after the Committee report, which went to such lengths to criticize Spindel and his activities, the wiretapper was the subject of a special article in *Life* magazine. In the issue of May 20, 1966, that magazine recorded Spindel's ingenuity and mentioned one particularly significant fact: "He has been indicted or arrested 204 times —all but twice for offenses connected with snooping—and beaten every rap but one. A jury in Springfield, Massachusetts, recently found him and a co-defendant guilty of eavesdropping. The fine, $500, has been suspended pending review."

The public record of wiretapping activities makes it clear that the same names appear over and over, with some of them linked to known private wiretap activities dating as far back as the 1930's.

New York has no monopoly on eminent wiretappers. In the nation's capital, the snooping exploits of Joseph W.

Shimon have often made headlines. Shimon, however, was not a private investigator like Broady, Gris, and Spindel. From 1929 to 1962, he was a member of the Washington, D.C., Metropolitan Police Force. As a police officer, he used wiretapping extensively. During his early years on the force, his tapping was limited to law-enforcement matters, but some of his later work smacked of private enterprise. In 1950, a subcommittee of the Senate District of Columbia Committee inquired into his activities. The airing of Lt. Shimon's activities exposed many points of disagreement among the witnesses, as well as some exceptional coincidences.

In 1940, Shimon had been transferred to the U.S. Attorney's office, to head a newly organized special investigating unit. In this job he had had no direct supervision by either the Metropolitan Police Department or the U.S. Attorney's office. Two years earlier, the Metropolitan Police had adopted a no-wiretap policy, but Shimon's new job presented him with an opportunity to demonstrate his flair for electronic snooping.

William Nolan, a business associate of Shimon, revealed that, in 1945, he drove Shimon to an apartment building in Washington where there was a wiretap plant in the basement. According to Nolan, Shimon had said the tap was on the telephone of Senator Josiah Bailey of North Carolina, Chairman of the Senate Commerce Committee. At the time, the Committee was holding hearings on a bill being supported by Pan American Airways and opposed by Trans World Airlines. Shimon flatly denied Nolan's testimony, and the conflict in their versions of Shimon's activities at that time could not be resolved.

Lt. Shimon's account of his post-1946 activities began

in the fall of that year when the Chief of Detectives in Miami, Florida, requested his help in locating a sugar swindler who was a fugitive from that state. Shimon was given a list of Washington telephone numbers which, it was believed, had been called by the fugitive. Shimon, posing as a telephone repairman, was able to get helpful information about these numbers from the telephone company. He tapped some of the telephones on this list, with the occasional assistance of Officer George Robison. In a sample tap, the last he installed from the Miami list, Shimon's special talents led him to the basement of the Occidental Hotel. He made suitable adjustments in the telephone installations there and then went to a room in the hotel for which he had registered earlier. He attached his monitoring equipment to the telephone wire in this room. With the assistance of Officer Robison, this tap was maintained for two or three weeks.

The telephone under surveillance belonged to Hugh Fulton, an attorney for TWA. Shimon told the Senate subcommittee that he had not known the identity of the subscriber until he read it in the newspapers in connection with the subcommittee's investigation. The tap, he said, revealed no information on the fugitive sugar swindler, so he had discontinued it. Because all his efforts had been unavailing, he had made no report to the Miami Chief of Detectives but, Shimon said, he had sent a bill for his expenses to Miami which had been paid. Prior to these hearings, the Miami Chief of Detectives had died, and a fire had destroyed many local police records. The subcommittee was therefore unable to verify Shimon's testimony.

Officer Robison's recollection was somewhat different.

According to him, Lt. Shimon had informed him at the time of the tap that the telephone belonged to Hugh Fulton, TWA's attorney. He said that Shimon had instructed him "to pay particular attention to any calls that would come in to Fulton from people that would be associated with the investigating committee on the Hill here, any conversations about any of the committees."

Shimon told of another case, in 1947, in which he had been sent to see Senator Owen Brewster of Maine. The Senator believed that someone was following him, and identified his shadower. The man was in the Senate Office Building at the time and Shimon followed him. The trail led to the Carlton Hotel, to a suite of rooms occupied by two attorneys for TWA. They were in Washington for hearings being conducted by the Senate War Investigating Committee. With the help of Officers John McHale and James Bryant, Shimon monitored the suite they occupied from an adjoining room. The attorneys later moved to the Mayflower Hotel, to which Shimon traced them. There he tried to place an induction coil near the attorneys' phone, but was unsuccessful. He told the subcommittee that he was not aware of the identity of the attorneys until the operation was already under way at the Mayflower.

The Senate committee that had been investigating the activities of Howard Hughes who controlled TWA, concluded its hearings on the same day that Shimon brought his own "hearings" at the Mayflower to an end. Senator Brewster was chairman of that committee. According to Shimon's testimony, none of his work had revealed any information concerning the reason Senator Brewster was being followed, and so he had never reported to the Senator. However, he said he did make arrangements to be reimbursed for his expenses.

Once again, the police officers who worked with Shimon had a different story to tell. They testified they had *not* received instructions concerning a man who followed Senator Brewster. Officers McHale and Bryant also testified that Shimon knew who the attorneys were. According to Bryant, Shimon had told him they were working on an investigation for the Senate or a Senate subcommittee, and that the U.S. District Attorney for the District of Columbia knew what they were doing. There were other conflicts in the testimony about Shimon's activities.

This man's superiors investigated his activities in 1949 and recommended that he be cited before the Police Trial Board. Also, a federal grand jury looked into his wiretap activities in 1950, but did not return an indictment. The Senate subcommittee report stated that one of the reasons for the failure of this grand jury to indict lay "in a strained and over-technical interpretation by the Justice Department and the United States district attorney . . . of the provisions of the Federal Communications Act."

Eventually, the Police Trial Board cleared Shimon of any wrongdoing in his tapping activities while he had been head of the special investigating unit. He was promoted to captain in 1954, and to inspector in 1960. Two years later he became involved in a widely publicized bugging of an attorney's room at the Mayflower Hotel, and was indicted and convicted on charges arising out of this incident. His conviction was reversed on appeal. Subsequently, he pleaded guilty to two misdemeanor charges related to the bugging, and avoided a new trial on the felony charge.

One of the major factors contributing to Shimon's success and to that of other private wiretappers has been the generous "look the other way" attitude of the telephone companies. While the companies dislike wiretapping, they dislike the publicity about it even more. For this reason, they often seem more anxious to project an image of telephone privacy than to preserve its actuality. It would seem that they are far more interested in public relations than in public welfare, and this conclusion is supported not only by their failure to file complaints with the authorities when taps are discovered but by their own use and sale of telephone-monitoring equipment.

As might be expected, specific abuses have been discovered in addition to the general monitoring by the telephone companies. In one case, reported to the Senate Subcommittee on Administrative Practice and Procedure by Joseph A. Beirne, President of the Communications Workers of America, members of his union discovered in Michigan that the company had used monitoring equipment for fourteen months to check the performance of an employee who was subsequently dismissed. The union contract had a provision that such monitoring would not be used for disciplinary purposes, and the case was forthwith brought to arbitration. In another case presented by Beirne, which took place in West Virginia, the home telephone of an employee was monitored at a time when it was known that a union official was with her, arranging to organize the operators. It was alleged that the tap was to determine if she was calling other operators to solicit union membership while they were on duty at the exchange.

The catalogue of activities enumerated here does the

barest justice to the story of private eavesdropping. From coast to coast, the techniques of snooping have appealed to persons with special interests in all walks of life. The average person, the everyday consumer, is a handy target. In 1957, a California committee uncovered several used-car dealers who had installed secret microphones in their sales offices. If a couple was considering a purchase, the prospective buyers were left alone in the bugged room at the most appropriate time to discuss the matter presumably in private. Armed with the information he had overheard, the salesman would then reappear to close the deal at the highest possible price within the purchasers' range. The committee also found that certain manufacturers used a similar device in convention display booths. The secret microphones allowed the manufacturers' representatives to hear frank reactions of the public to new products.

Not only as a consumer but as an employee, the average American may find himself the prey of the snooper. As we know, telephone monitoring is not the only means used to keep tabs on employees. One executive was so interested in what his personnel were doing and saying that he had a microphone installed in the toilet-tissue container in the ladies' room. A New York employer, carried away by a similar excess of interest, had a hidden camera installed in the men's room. And at a manufacturing plant in Baltimore, the management installed a closed-circuit TV surveillance system, with cameras located throughout the plant.

When, in 1936, Charlie Chaplin showed a somewhat similar situation in his movie *Modern Times,* the idea was so fantastic that everyone thought it very funny. It is no longer funny. In the particular case mentioned above the union representative warned the company that if the cameras were used, the workers would go out on strike. Apparently, this was successful in preventing the use of the system.

The lawyer and the businessman are also favorite targets. Consider the bugging of an attorney's room in Washington's Mayflower Hotel in 1962. This man represented El Paso Natural Gas Company, and was in the capital in connection with a proceeding before the Federal Power Commission. A short time earlier, another attorney for the same company had found a bug in his office in Beverly Hills, California. He had assumed it had something to do with a divorce case, until he learned of the Mayflower bug and another found in the office of a California public utility involved with El Paso Natural Gas Company in the FPC proceeding. This last bug was a transmitter placed under the public utility president's desk.

The utility executive who was the subject of this special snooping is only one of the many businessmen today who feel the need for—and who can afford—regular searches of their offices. One California private investigator, in the fall of 1965, said that he had two agents who spent three-quarters of their time doing such counter-snooping. His firm regularly checked the offices of some fifty lawyers. During 1965, they had found four active transmitters, two in lawyers' offices, one in a residence, and one in an executive office of a manufacturing plant. In his opinion, an eavesdropper might be paid as much as $10,000 for planting a transmitter and a telephone bug in the office of a prominent person.

Suppliers of snooping devices may find themselves playing on both sides of the same battleground, as do the snoopers themselves. A New York retail outlet sold snooping gear to a doctor who was having marital problems. Shortly thereafter, the doctor returned for some antispying equipment, convinced that his wife was doing to him what he was doing to her. Not much later, the wife came in to purchase her own antispying gear. This episode underlines a significant change in private snooping during the past few years: the ready availability of these devices, their low cost, and the relative simplicity of their operation have brought the practice within the reach of persons of limited means. This has increased the amount of private eavesdropping, and has made even more complicated the problem of trying to determine the extent of an already complex activity.

No one knows the extent of private snooping going on in America today. A number of studies and surveys shed some light on the problem, but the surreptitious and unethical (if not uniformly unlawful) nature of the activity makes full disclosure unlikely.

During the summer of 1965, William Shaw published the result of one such survey in the magazine *Law and Order*. His article examined the use of electronic devices by business and industry for security and internal management purposes. Representatives of 106 industrial, laboratory and business office organizations were interviewed. Of these, 87 companies were willing to provide information. Out of 55 industrial organizations, only 9 admitted they had used eavesdropping techniques. Six had equipment to monitor employee telephone conversations, but none did so on a full-time basis. Three of the industrial companies said they had used eavesdropping equipment in washrooms and lounge areas, and one had once tried to use a transmitter in a conference room.

Of the 14 retail stores that provided information in this survey, 9 indicated they had used hidden microphones in washrooms and dressing rooms, but only 4 used them on a regular basis. None of the stores admitted the use of wiretaps.

Only 3 of 11 laboratory organizations admitted the use of snooping equipment, but the 3 indicated they had used telephone monitoring, hidden microphones, and "other devices."

The last group questioned was composed of 7 business-office organizations. Unlike most of the other companies whose administrators were interviewed, none of these had security departments. For any security measures, they relied on building superintendents. Two of the organizations said they had used telephone monitoring on occasion, and 3 said that, while they had no such equipment, they had allowed their employees to believe that such equipment was in use.

Of the security people interviewed, a majority indicated that listening in on an employee's telephone calls without a specific reason is of questionable value. Most felt that spying merely for the sake of spying can cause more trouble than it is worth. They also felt that hidden microphones in washrooms and lounge areas are a low blow to employees. A few expressed the opinion that information obtained by such means supplied the snooper with more entertainment than information relevant to company business.

The survey concluded that snooping by private business is less extensive than exposé writers make it appear, but the writer readily admitted there is no way to prove this. He reached his conclusion on two grounds: (1) businessmen would not spend the money necessary for electronic snooping unless it could result in a provable monetary gain, and (2) businessmen are aware that their company's public image could be blackened by any revelation of snooping.

The survey made no mention of industrial espionage, and thus ignored one major area where electronic snooping is rife. All business firms must keep track, in some degree, of what their competitors are doing. Some companies limit their interest in this area to reading trade journals and newspapers, discussing competitors with customers, and "shopping" in competitors' establishments. But some have gone so far as to establish formal intelligence operations to keep an eye on their competitors and, in these instances, they often cross the line into the area of industrial espionage.

In 1962, *Industrial Research,* a trade magazine, conducted a survey of industrial espionage. An interesting paradox was reported: nearly everyone questioned thought that wiretapping was dangerous, and "dirty pool," yet one-third of the firms with formal intelligence operations reported they tapped phones or hired someone to do it for them. Another third of these firms carefully refused to say whether they did or did not tap.

The most tempting target for industrial spies is the Board of Directors' room, but the research laboratory is not far behind. The survey found that research firms do a lot of snooping, with more than half the larger firms carrying on formal programs of technical espionage. Some companies even maintain a network of efficient stool pigeons and thieves. *Industrial Research* reported that, in an increasing number of firms, the vice president for planning may be more interested in other companies' planning than in his own.

Not all industrial espionage is carried out by electronic means. Not only may certain primitive but presumably effective methods be used, but almost every "cloak and dagger" technique ever devised has been adapted in some way for industrial espionage. One company installed a false ceiling with peepholes in a room used for union meetings. Arrangements have been made with janitors and cleaning people to purchase the contents of a competitor's waste basket. Secretaries of key executives have been wooed. Blackmail, bribery, and burglary have all been used. And one widely used tactic of proven effectiveness is the planting of a spy in a competitor's business.

By all indications, there is an increasing use of the "lie detector" as a means of invading the privacy of the employee. A Dallas commercial polygraph firm gave 26,000 of these tests in 1963. The next year, the number increased by over fifty per cent. A Chicago firm gave 5,200 of these tests in 1964.

Retailers, faced with the problem of pilferage, are especially heavy users of the polygraph test. It is reported that one New York based chain employs two teams of roving testers who stage surprise visits to stores, line up employees, and begin firing questions. An executive of one commercial polygraph firm has said that almost every big company uses the so-called lie detector occasionally. Some use it as a regular part of their employment process to eliminate "bad risks." Labor unions have sought contract provisions that prohibit such tests of employees, and have campaigned for legislation against the polygraph.

A lie detector does not always detect lies and, because of this lack of reliability, courts have traditionally refused to admit its results as evidence. In questions of admissibility of evidence, there is no exception even if the person tested has submitted voluntarily to the test. Arbitrators of labor disputes have tended to follow the courts, but in recent years more emphasis is being given to the right-of-privacy issue involved.

The picture today looks discouraging, but it can be improved substantially if enough people begin to exercise their rights and their responsibilities. Where the right of privacy does not exist, a real show of interest on the part of potential victims could inspire state legislatures to create such a right. It might also inspire law-enforcement officials not only to enforce the law but to obey it.

Myron Brenton, discussing the right of privacy in the *Virginia Law Weekly,* in 1964, made this comment: "Those eager to stop the encroachments on our privacy must take the chance, the risks. Otherwise the privacy invaders won't have to take any. They will win—by default."

11

A Call for Action

In 1950, J. Edgar Hoover told a Congressional committee: "I dare say that the most violent critic of the FBI would urge the use of wiretapping technique if his child were kidnaped and held in custody."

Under these extreme circumstances such a critic, concerned only with the safety of his child, might also urge mass arrests, the use of vigilantes, and the third degree. He is not likely to worry, in the given situation, if the rights of others are trampled on. Even Thomas Jefferson or James Madison might have wavered under such pressures, and it is for this reason among others that we have courts, laws and a Constitution. A civilized society cannot leave it up to the victim of a crime to seek personal justice, retribution, and vengeance. Nor can a free society leave it to the victim to determine what methods should be used in enforcing the law.

Policemen and other law-enforcement officers share with the victims of crime a direct personal involvement in the apprehension and conviction of criminals. And civilization has learned the hard way that a free society cannot give a free hand to the policeman any more than to the wronged private citizen. Despite all this hard-won knowledge, the use of wiretapping, bugging, and many other privacy-invading techniques has, for the most part, been left up to policemen, government officials, or other persons who have a direct interest in the fruits of the invasion.

The effects of this policy on individual privacy have been mentioned often in these pages. But the individual whose privacy has been invaded has not been the only one harmed. The invaders, as well as law enforcement itself, have suffered. Here are the words of Justice Felix Frankfurter, in the On Lee case: "It is a quarter century since this Court . . . refused to put wiretapping beyond the constitutional pale where a fair construction of the Fourth Amendment should properly place it. Since then, instead of going from strength to strength in combating crime, we have gone from inefficiency to inefficiency, from corruption to corruption. The moral insight of Mr. Justice Brandeis unerringly foresaw this inevitability."

Justice Frankfurter's assessment of the situation is even more apt today, more than a decade later. The device used to incriminate On Lee was primitive compared with the space-age equipment now in use.

Two recent stories emphasize how present policy has led not only to the invasion of privacy but to the corruption of government officials. In 1964, as has already been recounted here, Thomas Bolan, attorney for Roy Cohn in a criminal case, discovered that his mail was subject to a cover. He immediately asked for a pretrial hearing on the use of mail covers.

The Assistant U.S. Attorney in the case filed a sworn statement in which he said that the U.S. Attorney's office had nothing to do with the placing of the cover. His statement was carefully phrased, so that it related only to the specific cover that had become known to Bolan. Attached to this statement was an affidavit from the Postal Inspector in charge of New York, swearing to the same facts. On the stand, the Postal Inspector reaffirmed his statement that the U.S. Attorney's office had nothing to do with the mail cover on Bolan.

The day after this statement had been made, the court asked the Assistant U.S. Attorney point-blank: "Did you ever obtain any information as a result of a mail watch?" The attorney, who had ordered a mail cover in September through a subordinate postal inspector, was not prepared to lie outright to the court. He admitted that he had. This led to a complete disclosure of the mail covers used against Bolan and Cohn.

The March, 1963, cover, which was the one discovered by Bolan, had been installed at the request of the IRS, but in September a similar request had been made by the U.S. Attorney's office. Because the second request had been made orally, the postal inspector in charge had no knowledge of it. In this case, an assistant U.S. Attorney walked a tightrope between truth and perjury to conceal his own part in a mail cover. Although his statement was technically accurate, there can be no question that it was his intent to deceive the court.

A few months prior to the Cohn case, another story involving an even higher level distressed many people with its implications of shaky government morality.

On September 23, 1963, the State Department notified Otto Otepka, Chief of the Evaluation Division of the Office of Security, that it proposed to dismiss him for actions unbecoming an officer of the Department. These actions had to do with alleged cooperation by Otepka with the Senate Internal Security Subcommittee which was then investigating State Department security procedures. In the Department's view Otepka provided improper assistance to the Senate's investigators. Over the next weeks, this Subcommittee released testimony that John F. Reilly had been appointed Deputy Assistant Secretary of State for Security in 1962, and that, before long, he had begun to suspect Otepka, one of his subordinates, of passing on information to the Senate Subcommittee. To verify these suspicions, Otepka's "burn bag" was periodically examined, without his knowledge. (This bag is the container in which all disposable classified material is placed, so that it can be burned.) An attempt was made to adjust the wiring in Otepka's telephone so that the receiver would serve as a permanent microphone, but the adjustment proved defective. Tapes of the suspect's telephone conversation were recorded, however.

When he learned of the tap on his phone, Otepka informed the Subcommittee. Reilly was called before the Subcommittee, as were his Special Assistant, David J. Belisle, and the Department's Chief of the Division of Technical Services, Elmer Dewey Hill. All three men denied ever having engaged in the tapping or bugging of employees. Each was asked specifically about Otepka's telephone, and each denied ever having tapped it or having it tapped.

Several weeks after this testimony, these men were directed by the Secretary of State to prepare letters clarifying and amplifying their testimony. These letters gave in detail the story outlined earlier here, but denied that any conversations had been intercepted. The Subcommittee found it hard to accept the differences in fact between the letters and earlier testimony as clarification and amplification. Accordingly, the three officials were asked to reappear.

Both Reilly and Belisle maintained that their earlier testimony was correct. They went down the line of questions to show how they had answered each one truthfully. This tour de force was achieved by giving an ingenious technical interpretation of each question. Belisle had not revealed the tap, he said, because he was out of town when it was in use and had only heard of it after his return. All his information, therefore, was only hearsay, and he claimed that he was not required to relate such knowledge. Reilly, for his part, said he considered his questioning in the nature of a cross-examination, and was required to answer only the specific questions asked. He could not be expected to volunteer information beyond the question. Hill, in contrast to the other two, admitted that he had answered some questions incorrectly because he had believed it his duty to the Department.

Here again we run into the old story of tightrope walking, or near perjury, by government officials who are trying to cover up participation in a snooping situation. In addition to the incidents of the burn-bag cover, and the wiretap, it was later revealed in the hearings that the combination on Otepka's safe had been cracked. This was done on Reilly's instructions by a technician using special equipment. The technician had turned over the combination to Reilly, who had gone to Otepka's office on a Saturday, opened the safe, and examined its contents.

Both stories clearly show the reluctance of government officials to admit publicly that they use privacy-invading techniques. The incidents also show the extremes to which these officials will go to hide their recourse to these techniques. In the legal vacuum that still exists, there is a great temptation to resort to such methods if they will help to "get your man." Adding to the temptation is the fact that the use of the techniques is not likely to be discovered. As a result, government officials sometimes find themselves stooping to these practices with little or no justification, and they make every effort to avoid disclosure. Their actions may not have been illegal but they know them to be wrong and, to avoid public censure, they compound the wrong by perjury or near perjury.

In each of the situations recounted here, government officials have found themselves in embarrassing and untenable positions because of the use of snooping techniques. There can be no denying, on the basis of this and additional evidence, that action is needed to clarify the right of privacy; it must be determined under what circumstances invasion of privacy may be permitted. The individual needs such action to secure his right to be let alone. The law-enforcement officer needs definitive action to clarify the limits of his authority. And society at large needs action on both counts: to protect personal privacy and to promote effective law enforcement.

The Supreme Court will undoubtedly continue to defend the right of privacy in the cases that come before it.

Many techniques now widely used may, in time, fall under the provisions of the Fourth Amendment.

By the very nature of our system of government, however, the Court alone cannot meet the needs of the American people in this situation. It does not possess the power to initiate action. Also, it is bound by certain rules that limit what questions it can decide even in those cases that come before it. Section 605 of the Federal Communications Act is a good example. The Court has not re-examined Olmstead, nor has it decided the question of the legality of tapping. This is because of 605 and its wording. Thus, while the Supreme Court can be expected to produce significant future action in securing and defending privacy, and in determining the propriety of law-enforcement practices, it cannot provide any immediate solutions to the current problem.

The Executive branch, on the other hand, is in a position to take immediate action: it can cause its employees to cease and desist from these practices. Yet it is unlikely to do so despite the specific instructions of the President. As pointed out earlier, several steps have been taken to curb the offensive practices, most of which are temporary in character. A new Postmaster General, a new Secretary of the Treasury, or a new Internal Revenue Commissioner could easily undo what has been done. And in any case, how much real meaning—in the sense of permanence—is there in rules issued by agency chiefs? The IRS, for example, has had a regulation banning wiretapping since 1938, yet as we know it has sent its agents to a wiretap school, and its national office has provided wiretap equipment as well as the agents to install it. Certain agencies, the

FDA among them, have refused even to recognize the possibility that some of their actions may be censorable, despite the use of all types of electronic gear and privacy-invading techniques. The current situation has come about because the use of wiretapping, eavesdropping, and similar techniques has not been strongly and consistently discouraged within the Executive branch of government. Because the interest of the law-enforcement official is too direct and personal, any equable solution to this situation will have to come from outside the Executive branch.

Unlike the other two branches of government, the Congress suffers no disabilities in approaching the problem. It can take the initiative, and it is not directly involved in day-to-day law enforcement. Further, it can establish national policy applicable to government agents as well as private citizens. There is one area in which the effectiveness of Congressional jurisdiction appears doubtful: the use of wired bugs and recorders by private citizens. The states alone have clear authority to ban such practices. To cooperate fully with Congress in controlling and finally eliminating private snooping, the states would have to establish general control over the use of lie detectors and so-called psychological tests, as well. State legislation is therefore needed to arrive at the total solution.

Despite the ability of Congress to initiate legislation to protect privacy, it has taken no such action since 1934, even though the intent of Section 605 has clearly been thwarted by the Justice Department interpretations. Efforts to enact wiretap legislation have simply exposed the battle lines in the continuing conflict between those who champion privacy and law-enforcement interests. It may be hoped that the disclosures of the Senate Subcommittee on Administrative Practice and Procedure will convince Congress it can no longer postpone action to protect the individual's right to privacy.

Admittedly, there is no ready-made solution for the problem. It is not possible to start down the list of devices and practices and say, "This one is O.K., but that one is not." Many devices have legitimate uses. A miniature transmitter, for instance, may be used to summon assistance in an emergency. Some practices have little effect singly, but may become serious threats to privacy when joined with others. Many government agencies, for example, obtain information on citizens in the course of administering federal programs. There is nothing wrong with this. But if all this information were fed into one electronic dossier bank, as has been proposed, a threat to individual privacy of unimaginable proportions would be raised.

Other considerations in the quest for solutions concern the indispensability of certain practices and the available alternatives. The mail cover, the pen register, and the telephone company toll slip all provide the same type of information. They reveal to the government the particular person or persons with whom a suspect is communicating. All three practices restrict personal freedom of communication. They interfere not only with privacy but with freedom of speech. Today, the use of these techniques by government agents is routine.

James Madison once wrote a word of advice to those who would argue that the invasion of privacy caused by these practices is too slight to be of concern: "The people of the United States owe their Independence and their liberty, to the wisdom of descrying in the minute tax of three pense on tea, the magnitude of the evil comprized in the precedent. Let them exert the same wisdom, in watching against every evil lurking under plausible disguises, and growing up from small beginnings. Obsta Principiis."

A mail cover should not be authorized, except in the most serious criminal cases. Court orders should be required or, as an alternative, the specific approval of the Postmaster General, based on written request.

The pen register is of limited value in law enforcement when compared with the degree of its invasion of privacy. Its use should be banned, except by the telephone company in its overt routine operations.

Toll slips should be available to law-enforcement officials on the service of a summons or subpoena only.

The polygraph, or so-called lie detector, appears to serve only as a psychological blackjack. All use of this dubious instrument of Inquisition should be discontinued by federal agencies unless and until extensive and irrefutable scientific evidence of its value is forthcoming. If that day should ever arrive, then its usefulness should be reconsidered.

Psychological tests should not be used by federal agencies except where a doctor-patient relationship exists. The need to screen government personnel does not justify the serious intrusion on privacy that results from such testing, particularly when there still exists a gap in the correlation of test results and job performance.

Wiretapping and bugging pose by far the most serious and ubiquitous threats to privacy, and they also provide the most ready assistance to law enforcement. The wide private use of these techniques raises further problems but these are relatively easy to solve, at least legally.

It has consistently been claimed that wiretapping is necessary for national security. The argument is also advanced that wiretapping provides the only means to reach the organized crime chiefs who insulate themselves from the activities of their underlings. But it is clear from available evidence that spies, and those in the higher echelons of organized crime, are too smart to discuss their activities on the telephone. Actually, the primary value of wiretapping in these instances seems to be to provide miscellaneous information. A tap on a suspected spy or crime chief will allow officers to keep track of the subject's whereabouts and general activities, but it usually yields little information of value in solving or preventing specific crimes. Wiretapping is primarily useful in catching such lesser fry as gamblers, prostitutes, dope peddlers, and similar law-breakers who may or may not be linked to organized crime.

FBI Director J. Edgar Hoover, in 1940, described wiretapping as an "archaic and inefficient" practice which "has proved a definite handicap or barrier in the development of ethical, scientific, and sound investigative techniques."

In his dissent on the On Lee case, Justice Frankfurter lumped electronic snooping with such unsavory practices as the third degree, and search without warrant. He said, also: "My deepest feeling against giving legal sanction to such 'dirty business' . . . is that it makes for lazy and not alert law enforcement. It puts a premium on force and fraud, not on imagination and enterprise and professional training."

Here are two major voices that question the intrinsic *value* of such aids to law enforcement generally, not to mention their effect on privacy.

Yet the Supreme Court's decision in the Olmstead case that wiretapping is not subject to the Fourth Amendment is still controlling. Even the most ardent advocates of law-enforcement wiretapping have come around in recent years to the view that this practice is a serious invasion of privacy. Attorney General Kennedy, as has been noted earlier, told the Senate Judiciary Committee in 1962 that "wiretapping in some respects involves a greater invasion of privacy than does a search." It is largely because of this attitude that no serious effort has been made in Congress since 1954 to authorize wiretapping without requiring court orders. Attorney General Kennedy's 1962 bill called for the right to wiretap in national security cases without court orders, but this provision was doomed from the start.

It is maintained by some that the requirement for court orders meets all the privacy problems raised by wiretapping. They draw an analogy between a search warrant and a wiretap court order. However, there are several obvious differences between the two. Chiefly, the search warrant is known to the victim, and he may go into court and challenge it. Also, the executor of the warrant must make a return to the court to show what use was made of the authority granted by it. But a wiretap court order would never be known to the victim unless some use was made of the information so obtained. For this reason, it would take a considerable length of time before the order could be challenged. In most cases, the victim would probably never know of the tap.

Most proposed court-order systems have not called for a return, but even if they did, few judges would have the time to read a 30-, 60-, or 90-day transcript, or listen to the tapes. One of James Otis's primary objections to the writ of assistance granted to customs officials before our Revolutionary War was that they required no return. The government agent was therefore free to make what use he wanted of the writ. Judge Samuel Hofstadter, of New York, used to require that a written report be submitted to him on the results of wiretap orders he granted. He found little in these reports, he said, to prove that the taps had achieved any valuable purpose.

Justice Robert H. Jackson, in his book *The Supreme Court in the American System of Government,* raised a point about court-order wiretapping that has been almost completely ignored:

> . . . perhaps the most significant . . . limitation upon the judicial power is that this power extends only to cases and controversies. . . . [Its] only power is to decide lawsuits . . . and its only method of proceeding is by the conventional judicial, as distinguished from legislative or administrative, process. . . . It also precludes imposition on federal constitutional courts of non-judicial duties. Recent trends to empower judges to grant or deny wiretapping rights to a prosecutor . . . raise interesting and dubious questions. A federal court can perform but one function—that of deciding litigations—and can proceed in no manner except by the judicial process.

Another major problem not solved by the court-order advocates is the fact that tapes can be doctored. A tape introduced in evidence carries great weight with a jury. After all, they listen to the actual voice of the defendant, engaged in incriminating conversation. But it is quite possible to alter a tape so that the change cannot be detected even with electronic equipment. Sentences, phrases, words, and even syllables can be cut out and moved around, and the person can be made to "say" whatever the technician wishes him to say.

Here, now, are suggestions for a solution to the problem of wiretapping:

All private wiretapping should be prohibited. Both tapping and divulgence should be considered crimes.

One party to a call should be permitted to have a third party listen in or record the call, provided any other party or parties to the call are given notice.

Law-enforcement officers should be allowed to tap with the consent of one party to the conversation, under specified conditions. With such consent, they should be able to listen to or record a telephone conversation, provided they have obtained a court order. Here, the order could and should be limited to specific conversations, and to conversations that constitute a crime or may reasonably be expected to be an integral part of a crime. The other requirements for obtaining a search warrant should also be met. This would provide law enforcement with an important tool in gambling, prostitution, and narcotics investigations without lessening the powers of the Fourth Amendment to protect privacy. Evidence obtained should be admissible in court.

Where a person is the victim of a kidnaper or extortionist, or offered a bribe, law-enforcement officers should be allowed, with the victim's consent, to monitor telephone calls placed to him by the criminal, without court orders. However, an order should be obtained within twenty-four hours after the police receive notice of the crime. In this situation, again, the order could and should meet the requirements of the Fourth Amendment and the evidence should be admissible.

When neither party to the telephone call has consented, law-enforcement officers should be prohibited from wiretapping. Both interception and divulgence here, too, should be considered crimes.

In the court-order situations here indicated, provision should be made, where a prosecution is brought, to notify the subject of the tap that his conversation has been seized. This should be done in adequate time before trial for him to challenge the order. In all cases, returns should be made to the issuing judge without delay to inform him of the action taken under authority of his order. In view of its limited nature, the court should not have difficulty in reviewing the results.

In national security cases involving a clear danger, the President, as Commander-in-Chief, would have authority to order tapping, at least so long as the Olmstead decision remains in effect. Information so obtained would not be admissible in court. Should Olmstead be overruled at some future time, then the Constitution would require that national-security taps be subject to the same restrictions as other law-enforcement taps.

This recommended federal legislation should be made applicable to federal and state law-enforcement officers, and federal and state courts. It protects privacy to the full extent of the Fourth Amendment, and at the same time allows law-enforcement use of wiretaps in the crimes where the technique has proved most useful.

As for bugging, because few legislative efforts have been made to regulate it, less evidence has been presented to support the need for its use in law enforcement. It is claimed to be of value in the following situations:

To record bribe offers to government agents or public officials.

To record transactions, involving narcotics or other contraband, between undercover agents or informers and a suspect.

To record bets placed by undercover agents or informers, as well as conversations in suspected gambling centers.

To record spiels of "medicine men" or other sellers of fraudulent health products and devices.

To coordinate raids and arrests.

To provide protection for undercover agents and informers.

To maintain general surveillance of the home or office of a suspected criminal.

It would appear from all this that bugging is a useful law-enforcement tool. But it will be noted that in many of the situations listed here, the bug serves only to support the word of a government agent or informer. It hears no more than he can hear himself.

The possibility of court orders for bugging which meet the requirements of the Fourth Amendment also seems to be limited. A wiretap picks up all conversation on a specific wire, while a planted bug will pick up all conversation in a particular area. It is not possible to limit its seizure to a specific conversation, and even if it were, the conversation normally would only be evidence per se. Also, there is the problem of a continuing seizure. The Fourth Amendment seems to preclude the use of all bugs where a physical intrusion would necessarily accompany their installation. In any case, they are similar to the wiretap in that their use falls short of the demands of our democratic traditions.

Because of the jurisdictional gap, it is not possible for Congress alone to protect privacy against all electronic snoopers. But there is a suggested approach to the problem.

The use of electronic devices by law-enforcement officers and informers should be allowed with court orders if the government agent is a participant in the monitored conversation or has the consent of one party to the conversation. Requirements similar to those enumerated for wiretap court orders should be imposed. This would call for both federal and state legislative action.

Congress should ban the use of radio devices by private citizens to monitor private conversation, and the states should similarly prohibit the use of wired bugs and recorders. An exception should be provided where all parties to the conversation consent to the monitoring or recording. The prohibition must be limited to private conversations or it could seriously interfere with radio and television coverage of public events. Private conversations accidentally and unavoidably heard under these circumstances would also be exempted. Again, both monitoring and divulgence should be considered crimes.

Telephone companies should be barred from leasing lines to government agencies for wiretapping or bugging. Advertisement of snooping devices should be prohibited. (Miniature recorders and transmitters have legitimate uses, and their advertisement for such purposes is entirely proper. But there is no reason to allow them to be promoted for private spying and snooping.) Manufacturers and distributors of such surveillance equipment should be licensed and their distribution regulated. It may be too early to tell if there is any value in extending licensing to owners of this kind of equipment. In view of the ease with which home-made devices of this kind can be put together, a licensing program might prove to be more trouble than it is worth. The experience of Maryland with its new law of this type should provide some facts on which to base a decision.

One final measure that should be considered by Congress is the framing of a Code of Conduct for federal investigators. This code would set out the do's and don't's in their relations with, and treatment of, both suspects and third parties. A code of this kind would have to be drawn up with extreme care so as not to interfere unnecessarily with the investigator's initiative. Actually, with adequate education programs and supervision, such a statutory code might not be necessary. This is especially likely if provision were made for all federal agency manuals to be reviewed by an independent authority, such as the Chairman of the Permanent Administrative Conference once he is appointed.

These recommendations do not cover all possible situations in which wiretaps and bugs may be used. Nor do they exhaust all ideas for control and regulation. But they suggest an approach that seems compatible with the Fourth Amendment and our democratic traditions, while recognizing the needs of law enforcement.

In addition to the above, the civil law should not be neglected in its capacity to protect the right of privacy against the intrusions noted here. It is recommended that each state survey its own civil law in this area. Legislation should be enacted to establish a comprehensive and actionable right of privacy, including punitive damages for any abuse of this right.

If the currently intensified war on privacy is to be stopped—or even slowed down—one final step is necessary: the full commitment of the American people. On this point, the Special Committee on Science and Law of the Association of the Bar of the City of New York, issued a call to arms on November 15, 1965: "[It] requires that our businessmen, our district attorneys, our journalists, our men of science—to mention only a few—be concerned with the human claim to privacy, as well as with their dominant respective concerns for the profitable enterprise, the enforcement of society's laws, the freedom of the press and the freedom of science."

The time has passed when the Congress, the legislatures of the states, and the American people can afford the luxury of ignoring the situation. In March, 1966, Attorney General Katzenbach sent up a signal before a Senate committee to indicate just how bad the wiretapping situation has become under present law. Unless Congress could reach agreement on the authorization of limited law-enforcement tapping, he said, he felt that it (and private wiretapping) should be prohibited. He asked for a single exception to this blanket prohibition: Presidentially authorized taps in national-security cases. This statement reversed the long-standing policy of the Justice Department in tacit and at times overt support of law-enforcement wiretapping.

The Attorney General's statement is one more admonition, telling us that the house of individual privacy so carefully constructed by the men who founded our country is on fire. The time to take action is today, because tomorrow may be too late.

The last words must once more be those of Justice Louis Brandeis, writing in 1928:

"The makers of our Constitution undertook to secure conditions favorable to the pursuit of happiness. They recognized the significance of man's spiritual nature, of his feelings, and of his intellect. They knew that only a part of the pain, pleasure, and satisfaction of life are to be found in material things. They sought to protect Americans in their beliefs, their thoughts, their emotions, and their sensations. They conferred, as against the Government, the right to be let alone."